Contents

I am grateful to Kim Paleg and Matt McKay for trusting me to give the teacher's perspective and for allowing me the opportunity to be part of their hope for the parents of tomorrow. A warm thank-you to Kayla Sussell, our editor and guide. Thanks to Greg and Will for supporting me in every way. Thanks to my extended family (Klein and Loy) for sharing time with this book. Thank you Mousse Sisters and sisters of the Assistance League of San Mateo County for your encouragement.

Introduction

After reading Dr. Paleg's book, *Kids Today, Parents Tomorrow,* I realized it has great potential for use in a variety of educational settings. This teacher's guide was created to facilitate the use of her book in secondary level courses. It offers educators ways to teach skill standards in the area of parenting and relationship skills.

Kids Today, Parents Tomorrow is the book we've all been waiting for. It contains the new paradigms for understanding parenting and relationship skills. In the past, family life educators worked with concepts that were far more theoretical than practical. For example, when working with the unit "Building Relationships," a teacher might present activities to explore theories about how relationships develop (The Wheel Theory, The Path of Intimacy, etc.), accompanied by strategies to encourage discussion about relationship issues such as respect, honesty, and commitment. Programs rarely emphasized the development of practical skills such as anger management or the components of nurturing.

Educators were influenced by many factors that emphasized relationship and parenting theory rather than skills development. For one thing, there didn't seem to be a great need to teach relationship skills. As evidenced by their speech and behavior, most students seemed to be receiving socialization (social skills training) on an everyday basis from their families. Furthermore, and probably even more significant to educators, there just weren't many sources of research-based information and strategies aimed at teaching relationship and parenting skills. Lastly, we have to admit to our dependence on the tradition of educational institutions that assigns every teacher the role, "Sage on Stage." For a long time, we had the luxury of practicing educational methods that allowed us to stand and profess our vast knowledge while students sat quietly and listened.

Dr. Paleg's book arrives at the perfect time to help us keep pace with the new demands that are being placed on education today. Currently, social and economic strains on the family are requiring schools to supplement the socialization training that students receive from their families with the teaching of relationship and parenting skills. The federal government formalized these expectations in the SCANS Report (*The Secretary's Commission on Achieving Necessary Skills*, U.S. Dept. of Labor publication, June 1991).

Finally, we all know that lecture-based teaching strategies are not as effective as they used to be. Dr. Paleg's book is the product of recent research findings and responds to the much-discussed need to be more effective as parents and in all of our relationships. Her book provides the information we have needed to shift to inquiry-based teaching and to an emphasis on skills development.

Kids Today, Parents Tomorrow is flexible and can be fitted into any style of curriculum, integrated or single-subject. Dr. Paleg's goal is to provide working models for parental speech and action that are likely to produce effective results. The objective of the teacher's guide is to provide ready-to-use strategies to draw the student into an exploration of these skills. The level of skill achieved by students depends first on their ability to grasp the ideas presented, and then to practice those ideas in their real lives.

For teachers the title, *Kids Today, Parents Tomorrow*, provokes a not-so-subtle reality check. The reality is that today we are teaching "kids." Roughly translated, that means the future is Friday, the objective is to have fun, and it won't happen to me! Motivating "kids" to learn parenting skills can be tough because *our* objectives don't match *their* objectives! We want them to prepare for real-life responsibilities like money management and parenthood while they want to build friendships and party. We will probably be more successful if we respect their interests and sell them on the idea that, *by practicing the skills taught in Dr. Paleg's book, they can have better relationships today!* After all, parenting is one kind of relationship and, basically, all relationships require the same interpersonal skills. So, here's your mantra, "Everything you learn in this lesson will help you build all kinds of relationships." Say it often and loudly.

How to Use
This Guide

Why We Have a Teacher's Guide

This Teacher's Guide was created to conserve your time and energy. We want to make it easy for you to use *Kids Today, Parents Tomorrow*.

Kids Today, Parents Tomorrow
Was Written for You

Kids Today, Parents Tomorrow and the teaching strategies in the Teacher's Guide were designed for use in existing or new high school courses. This program is especially appropriate for school-age parent programs. It can also be adapted for use in parenting courses offered by community colleges, adult education courses, city recreation departments, and educational services offered by HMOs and hospitals.

The Teaching Goal of *Kids Today, Parents Tomorrow*

Dr. Paleg wrote *Kids Today, Parents Tomorrow* to provide readers with information about alternative ways to respond to everyday relationship issues that can result in more effective parenting and relationship interactions. Comprehension, therefore, is not enough! Readers are asked to *apply* the material to their own lives by *practicing* more effective relationship and parenting skills. Hopefully, the teaching strategies in this Guide will facilitate comprehension and enable students to make the leap from reading to practice.

How the Teacher's Guide Is Organized

The Teacher's Guide gives you five kinds of help for each chapter. They are as follows:

Chapter Overview

Teaching Strategies

Handout Masters

Overhead Projection Masters

It is important that the teacher read each chapter in the student reader before reading the corresponding Chapter Overview and Teaching Strategies.

Chapter Overview

The first step in teaching a lesson is to survey the "landscape" of the information you plan to present. The first section of each chapter does that task for you. The chapter concepts have been "mapped out" for you in the following ways:

- *Goal*—Explains what the author hopes the reader will gain from the chapter.

- *Objectives*—Explains what the teacher hopes the students will learn from the chapter lesson.

- *Rationale*—Describes why this is an issue worthy of our teaching and learning efforts.

- *Essential Questions and Answers*—These are the questions that frame the concepts presented in the chapter and guide our inquiry throughout the lesson.

The answers are the basic knowledge that learners will internalize during the lesson.

- *Resources*—Places to go for additional information, supplies, and materials.

Students learn better when they know what, why, and how they are learning. Most of the information provided in each Chapter Overview should be presented to students before and during the lesson.

Teaching Strategies

This section presents a variety of strategies designed to provoke thought and skill development relating to the chapter concepts. The strategies presented here try to engage learners in increasingly more sophisticated levels of investigation and understanding of the content. Note that when you are reading the teacher's instructions for each strategy, it would be helpful to refer to the handout or overhead for that activity. This will clarify the instructions. Teaching strategies are organized in the following way:

- *Quickies and Openers*—The first teaching strategies presented for most chapters are quickies and openers. These activities are used to introduce a unit or a lesson concept, engage student attention, or to remind students of what they've been studying after a long weekend away from the subject. Quickies and Openers may be used to influence student thought and/or emotions (affective openers). In the classroom, we are trying to raise awareness of the way students perceive everyday issues. We are trying to arouse feelings of curiosity, interest, and motivation.

- *Knowledge*—These activities are designed to help readers remember and organize the concepts they read about in the chapter. One or more of the Knowledge activities for each chapter should be done either during the chapter reading or immediately after the chapter reading.

- *CAASE Work*—After a foundation of information is built by the *Knowledge*-gathering activity, *you may use some or all* of the CAASE work activities provided to further immerse the students in the chapter concepts. CAASE stands for comprehension, application, analysis, synthesis, and evaluation. These activities are designed to:

C—Check the learner's *comprehension* of the chapter material.

A—Show the student how the chapter concepts can *apply* and have meaning in their own lives by connecting newly learned concepts to past learning, associated thoughts, and feelings.

A—Cause the student to break down the material into its component parts to *analyze* and identify relationships between the parts.

S—Enable the student to create something new from the concepts learned. The *synthesis* of old and new concepts allows the student to project new concepts into future situations.

E—Challenge the student to judge or *evaluate* the material for a given purpose.

Many of these activities can be assigned as homework. This is also a great way to expose parents to the material and the purpose of your course.

Note: Many of the teaching strategies in this Guide are designed to incorporate communication skills, study skills, practice in different forms of writing, and exposure to cultural practices, arts, and crafts.

Levels of Ability: Each teaching strategy requires the learner to perform at different levels of ability. The level of thought required for each strategy is identified by the descriptive word to the right of its title. These words, "easy," "average," and "challenging" represent the following levels of difficulty:

- **Easy:** Participation in these strategies requires the learner to process knowledge by performing lower level thinking skills, such as recall, read, review, list, outline, and memorize.

- **Average:** Participation in these strategies requires the learner to comprehend and apply knowledge by performing higher level thinking skills, such as explain, reword, translate, illustrate, and construct.

- **Challenging:** Participation in these strategies requires the learner to analyze, synthesize, and evaluate knowledge by performing the highest level thinking skills, such as compare, deduce, forecast, design, compose, and assess.

Handout Masters

The Handout Masters section contains ready-to-duplicate handouts needed for the teaching strategies.

Overhead Projection Masters

These pages can be copied onto overhead transparencies to be used with an overhead projector. Students understand better when they hear *and* read instructions. Posting instructions throughout the activity eliminates questions and confusion. We need all the help we can get!

Answers

To save you time, the answers to some of the activities are given. These sheets can be copied on an overhead transparency to allow students to check their own work.

Assessing Student Outcomes: A Portfolio Project

One of the teaching strategies in each chapter is a performance task. A performance task is an important tool for assessing students' ability to perform the standards outlined in "Objectives." Upon completion of *Kids Today, Parents Tomorrow*, each student may complete ten performance tasks that can be kept as a Parenting Portfolio. You might even want to award a "Prepared for Parenting" certificate to each student who completes a portfolio. The last page in the Handout section is a sample "Prepared for Parenting" certificate.

The Parenting Portfolio may be kept by students for future reference. These projects may also be used in peer education workshops, as displays around campus, in Family, Career and Community Leaders of America activities, county fair exhibits, etc. They will provide great publicity for your course.

Chapter One

How to Nurture
Your Child

Chapter Overview

Goal

In this chapter you will learn how to provide emotional nurturing in all of your relationships. Special emphasis is placed on how to give emotional nurturing to children.

Objectives

At the end of this lesson you will

- Know the six essential components of nurturing

- Know how to provide the six essential components of nurturing

- Understand how nurturing promotes a child's healthy development

- Understand the role of nurturing in all relationships

Rationale

Providing good nurturing allows children to grow into responsible, mature adults with an accurate sense of their worth and value as human beings. Children learn how to nurture themselves when these skills have been modeled by their parents. People in all kinds of relationships thrive on nurturing.

Essential Questions and Answers

1. What is nurturing?

   Answer: To nurture is to provide support, encouragement, and nourishment.

2. What is physical nurturing?

   Answer: Physical nurturing involves caring for physical needs such as cuddling, food and drink, warm clothes, sleep, and being kept clean and safe from danger.

3. What is emotional nurturing?

   Answer: Nurturing that involves attending to a person's emotional needs, such as the need to be understood and accepted by others or the need to have self-esteem.

4. What are the six essential components of emotional nurturing?

   Answer:

   - Attention

   - "Mirroring"

   - Understanding

   - Acceptance and Respect for Who the Person Is

   - Soothing Pain

   - Fostering Self-Esteem

5. What benefits does a child (or any person) receive from emotional nurturing?

   Answer: Children gain a sense of their worth and value as human beings. As a result of parental modeling of nurturing behavior, children learn to nurture themselves and others.

6. How do we provide nurturing to others?

   Answer:

   - **Attention** means **spending time** with a child (playing, reading, talking, going for walks, etc.), **noticing** what the child is doing, saying, or needing, and **listen-**

ing when a child asks questions or talks to you. **Patience** is necessary to give the child time to speak or do something.

- **Mirroring** is practiced when we show children that they are wonderful and a pleasure to be around. It is practiced when we show delight in a child. It is communicated through facial expression, gesture, and tone of voice. It can also be verbally communicated.

- **Understanding** is practiced by listening to thoughts and feelings, likes and dislikes, needs and wants, hopes and dreams, and fears and fantasies, with the objective of **trying to get inside the other person's world in order to feel how it feels to them**. It is done without judgment.

- **Acceptance and respect** is given by people who accept the fact that we are all born with different temperaments and don't expect others to change. In a parent-child relationship, it is **accepting your child for who he or she is** and respecting those characteristics that make him or her special. It means **communicating acceptance and respect to the child**.

- **Soothing pain** means helping a child learn how to cope with the painful feelings and experiences of childhood by acknowledging that the experience hurts and allowing the child the opportunity to learn how to solve his or her own problems.

- **Fostering self-esteem** is practiced by:

  —Helping your child feel lovable and worthwhile by mirroring him or her as wonderful and lovable.

  —Providing focused attention by listening to and accepting your child's full range of feelings.

  —Expressing your own feelings honestly and appropriately.

  —Understanding and respecting the person your child really is.

  —Giving your child the freedom to grow and develop at his or her own pace.

  —Establishing discipline that includes clear, understandable, and consistent rules.

  —Establishing discipline that gives the child choices, consistent and appropriate consequences without anger, and problem-solving opportunities.

  —Praising.

  —Giving unconditional love.

7. What is emotional neglect?

Answer: Emotional neglect takes place when parents don't take an interest in the child, and do not talk to or hold the child.

8. In what ways can neglect affect a child?

Answer: Neglected children are not taught to value themselves. They have a hard time trusting others, and they often end up seeing themselves as unworthy of love and attention. They can have achievement problems, get into trouble with their teachers and the law, form bad relationships, and generally act in self-destructive ways.

Resources

- Before starting this lesson, you may want to review Maslow's Hierarchy of Needs. Discuss physical and emotional needs and how needs are met for children and adults.

- You may want to define and discuss "modeling" as an act of parenting.

- *The Essential Haiku*. Edited by Robert Hass. Hopewell, NJ: Ecco Press.

- *The Zen Haiku and Other Zen Poems* by J. W. Hackett. New York, NY: Japan Publications (USA Inc.).

Teaching Strategies

 **Assign chapter 1 reading (*Easy*)**

Quickies and Openers

 **Plant Parenthood (*Easy*)**

Purpose: To introduce the concept "nurture." To encourage an emotional response to this lesson (affect).

Instructions: Bring in two identical plants. Place the plants in front of the classroom where your students enter.

Use **Overhead 1**,

OR

Make a quick butcher paper or chalkboard chart like the one on the next page:

Plant Parenthood

Care?	How often?	What if it gets care?	What if it doesn't get care?

What is another word for care? <u>N   </u>

Ask the students the following questions and fill in their answers on the chalkboard chart:

- What care will these plants need to thrive?

- How often will the plants need each type of care?

- What might happen to the plants if they get all the care they need?

- What might happen to the plants if they do not get all the care they need?

- What is another word for this type of care that begins with "n"?

Because the entire nurturing lesson might take only a few days, you may want to start this affective opener a week or two in advance. Keep the plants in your classroom for the duration of this lesson. Give one the care prescribed by your students. Give the other plant no care.

Debrief in a week or two or when the neglected plant begins to look pitiful. *Discuss the different results and the analogy made between nurturing a plant and nurturing a child.* And then, please water that poor plant!

❤ Graffiti Wall (*Easy*)

Purpose: To raise awareness about all the ways we nurture each other.

Instructions: Have a huge piece of butcher paper taped up on a wall. Provide lots of colorful felt pens. Write the title "The Ways We Nurture Each Other" and the definition "Nurturing is to provide support, encouragement, and nourishment" at the top of the graffiti paper.
Have students come up to the wall and write all the ways we nurture our family and friends.

Debrief: Immediately. Discuss the fact that nurturing is critical to all relationships, critical to the healthy development of children, and that it is a *skill* we all benefit from learning and practicing.

❤ Current Events (*Easy*)

Purpose: To share knowledge and experiences about nurturing gathered from outside the classroom.

Instructions: Open class each day with one or more of the following questions. (Give time and attention to responses.)

- Did anyone observe an example of physical or emotional nurturing since our last class meeting?

- Did you hear anything on the news or read anything in the newspaper that is related to nurturing?

- Did anyone practice any form of nurturing in the last twenty-four hours?

- Was anyone the beneficiary of nurturing in the last twenty-four hours?

- Are you more aware of the role of nurturing in your relationships?

Knowledge

❤ Concept Wall (*Easy*)

Purpose: To review the six essential components of nurturing a child. To organize material read in the chapter.

Instructions: Roll out a ten-foot length of butcher paper. Quickly fold the chart into seven equal sections, draw lines, and label the chart as shown on the next page. Have it up on a wall before class begins.

Fill in the six essential components of nurturing a child during a *brief* class discussion. Then have your students number off from 1 to 7. OR if you have tables in your classroom, cut seven pieces of butcher paper 18" x 30," and pass one to each table. All the 1's are to find concepts in the chapter about the first essential component listed and write the concepts in the column below. You are looking for concepts that describe this type of nurturing and how parents perform it. Don't be shy . . . write down anything you find about that component. You will also need to fill in the lower portion which describes the positive benefits that a child gets from receiving this type of nurturing on a regular basis. Group 7 looks for concepts in the chapter that describe neglect. In the lower portion, group 7 lists the devastating effects that result from neglect.

You have ten minutes to finish the concept wall. Put up **Overhead 2** so that students can read the instructions as many times as needed to complete the activity.

When complete, tape all the pieces together on a wall to form one big poster (as shown below).

Debrief: Ask the question, "What are your observations about the six components of nurturing?" Hopefully, their observations will be that emotional nurturing requires time, patience, and effort on the part of the parent.

	Description		Devastating Effects
Neglect 7			
Fostering self-esteem 6		*In what ways does a child (or any person) feel good, thrive, or benefit by being nurtured in this way?*	
Soothing their pain 5			
Acceptance and respect for who they are 4			
Under-Standing 3			
Mirroring 2			
Attention 1			
Description			Benefits

OR

 ## The Beads of Oman (*Easy*)

Purpose: To review the six essential components of emotional nurturing. To provide a keepsake to remember that giving and receiving nurturing is how we build a wealth of relationships.

Materials Needed: A variety of lightweight, inexpensive wooden or glass beads with holes large enough to be strung on coated round elastic (plastic pony beads would do). Optional: Buy all silver and black or spray paint them silver in advance.

Four to six skeins of coated round elastic or just plain string; cut into 30″ lengths: one per student.

Thick cardboard that can be cut with scissors and folded

Heavy duty aluminum foil. Optional: Black tempera paint

3″ x 5″ cards trimmed down to 2½″ x 4″ (six per student)

Carbon paper

Scissors, glue, and possibly a stapler

Instructions: Read the instructions on **Handout 1** and make a sample silver box and necklace. You will need to demonstrate to the class how to make the silver jewel box. Handout 1 has a pattern and instructions for the silver jewel box to hold the note cards. **Overhead 3** gives instructions for making the note cards and the stringing of the jewel box and the beads. **Note:** The necklaces must be large enough to put on and take off over the head.

Tell the story of the beads of Oman to your students:

Oman, located in southeastern Arabia, exports dates and oil. Oil brought wealth to Oman; however, the people maintain many traditional customs and dress. One tradition, the display of personal wealth by wearing it, has continued among Oman's families. Women in Oman wear silver in the form of strung silver beads to show their family wealth.

Give these instructions to students: You will make your own beads of Oman today; however, instead of displaying your wealth, you will be making silver boxes which carry valuable reminders about nurturing.

Pass out Handout 1, materials, and put Overhead 3 on the projector.

OR

 Notetaking (*Easy*)

Purpose: Notetaking is a critical study skill. Students use three senses (hearing, touching, seeing) in addition to processing the information via summarizing and paraphrasing. During chapter reading and class lectures, notetaking helps students to organize and internalize information.

Instructions: Teach the notetaking technique explained on **Handout 2**. Use **Overhead 4** to demonstrate how to take notes.

OR

❤ Essential Questions (*Easy*)

Purpose: Asking these questions during or after the chapter reading will help students organize information about the six essential components of emotional nurturing.

Instructions: Use **Handout 3**.

CAASE Work

❤ Whodunit? (*Easy*)

Purpose: To have students practice understanding the six essential components of nurturing and how they are performed in our society.

Instructions: Use **Handout 4**. Students should be able to finish this activity in about fifteen minutes.

Debrief: Immediately. By having students recall past observations, this activity tests their understanding of nurturing. *Ask the class members to share five or six examples from their Handouts.* This discussion should be kept brief.

❤ Haiku (*Average*)

Purpose: To help students examine the role that nurturing has played in their own lives.

Instructions: Use **Handout 5**. The instructions are on the second page of the Handout.

Debrief: *Ask a few volunteers to read their poems to the class.* Mount them *all* on nice paper and display them in your classroom and in the school library.

What Time Is It? It's TV Time! (*Average*)

Purpose: This exercise gives students the opportunity to identify nurturing behaviors.

Instructions: Show an episode of a half-hour TV family sitcom. Have the students look for examples of nurturing and instruct them to take notes as they watch. In the larger part of their notes, on the right, they will write brief descriptions of the scenes that play out some form of nurturing. In the left-hand column, they can write the name of one of the six essential components of nurturing that is acted out in the scene. Use **Overhead 5** to post the instructions. Obviously, you will have to be a little picky about which episode you videotape. It will need to show lots of examples of nurturing! This could also be done as a homework assignment with the student deciding what to watch. If so, you may want to put up **Overhead 5** and have students copy the instructions onto the top portion of their notetaking paper.

Debrief by asking students to discuss the various examples of nurturing that occurred during a half-hour TV program. Use the terms from the chapter in your discussion: attention, mirroring, understanding, etc. Focus your discussion on **how** the nurturing was done (examine the component parts of nurturing).

 ## Nature/Nurture Display (*Challenging*)

Purpose: The student designs a "how-to" display to suggest **how** to practice nurturing.

Instructions: Use **Handouts 6** and **7**. **Handout 7** is the grading rubric for this assignment. By giving it to students in advance, they will know exactly how they are expected to perform on the assignment. **Note:** *There are a few grading rubrics and grade evaluation forms for some of the assignments. These are provided as models. It would not achieve the goal of this guide to spend the time necessary to produce a rubric or evaluation form for every teaching strategy contained herein. Also, all teachers have very personal approaches to evaluating student performance.*

Encourage students to produce beautiful displays. This will become their **Portfolio Project** and may be used for peer education. If you have decided to have your students compile portfolios, this may be the time to use **Handout 11** to explain the ongoing portfolio project.

Handout 6 instructs students to write similes. You will need to explain what a simile is.

A **simile** is a comparison stated with *like*, *as*, or *than* and sometimes with verbs such as *seems* or *appears*. The comparison must be between two different types of items. For example, the comparison "Town High seems just like my old school" is not a simile because two similar types of items are being compared.

Debrief: On the due date, take lots of time to allow everyone to see the displays shown on desktops. You may want to do peer evaluation: 1) Number the displays, 2) Students pick a number out of a hat, and 3) They use the rubric (**Handout 7**) to assess a display. Put the displays in display cases around school, in the library, in the main office, etc. Use them for public relations and peer education.

Role Play (*Challenging*)

Purpose: Students compose role plays to explore their understanding of *how* to perform nurturing.

Instructions: Organize students into dyads (two people). Pass out **Handout 8** to each dyad. Instruct students to refer to descriptions of the six essential components of nurturing from past assignments to write their role plays, OR pass out copies of the answer to Essential Question 6 from the chapter Overview; it's a good summary of the components. You can have each dyad write and perform one or more role plays, depending on how much time you have. You might want to tape videos of the role plays. The videos can be used for peer education.

Debrief: Immediately. The role play is the debriefing. Allow for a few clarifying comments; however, move right along or you'll be presenting role plays into the next millenium!

Editorial (*Challenging*)

Purpose: This challenges the student to examine nurturing, judge the value of nurturing, and promote the practice of nurturing children and others.

Instructions: Use **Handout 9**. Also give the students **Handout 10**, the rubric for the editorial, so they can complete the assignment to expected standards.

The editorials are the final assessment of student outcomes for this lesson. Use the rubric (Handout 10) to assess them. The completed editorials can be added to the nature/nurture display as instructed in Handout 9.

Debrief and Closure to Lesson: On the day that editorials are turned in, have each student choose their three favorite editorial arguments for nurturing and write them on a 3" x 5" card. Sit in a chair and enjoy a civilized *chat with your students about the importance of nurturing, the six components, the practice of nurturing in all types of relationships, and the benefits children receive from nurturing.*

Chapter Two

Finding and Reinforcing the Good

Chapter Overview

Goal

In this chapter you will learn that positive reinforcement of desired behavior is more effective than criticism of misbehavior. You will understand that positive reinforcement builds self-esteem and increases the person's desire to practice more acceptable behavior.

Objectives

At the end of this lesson you will

- Recognize the value of positive reinforcement over criticism in encouraging desired behavior in children and others

- Know some of the ways to reinforce others, especially with attention

- Know the four steps in finding and reinforcing good behavior

- Understand that using positive reinforcement builds a better relationship and makes people feel good about themselves

Rationale

There is a fairly widespread belief that if you criticize someone sufficiently he or she will work at improving themselves. Actually, criticism is more likely to erode a person's motivation and self-esteem.

Essential Questions and Answers

1. How do you encourage your children to behave better if the standard approach, focusing on their misbehavior, doesn't work?

   Answer: The key to encouraging your child (or anyone) to behave better is to find and reinforce their good behavior.

2. Why do so many parents resort to criticism in an attempt to correct misbehavior?

   Answer: There is a widespread belief in American culture that if you want someone to do better, you just have to focus on all the ways that they're not doing well enough. It's all too easy to get into a rut of constantly scolding, giving time-outs, and yelling "No."

3. What might be some of the outcomes of using criticism to correct misbehavior with children and in other relationships?

   Answer: Although there is occasionally some short-term improvement with this approach, the long-term result is more often a decrease in that person's self-esteem and a corresponding decrease in the motivation for doing better. Behavior that is reinforced with criticism probably will be repeated.

4. What is reinforcement?

   Answer: Reinforcement occurs when someone is rewarded for behaving in a particular way. After reinforcement people are more likely to behave in the same way again.

5. What is a reinforcer?

   Answer: A reinforcer is the reward that someone is given for a particular behavior. It is anything that increases the chances that a behavior will be repeated.

6. How does positive attention work as a reinforcer with adults and children? Give some examples of positive attention.

Answer: Behavior that is noticed or attended to is more likely to be repeated than that which is ignored. Examples of positive attention include a smile, a wink, a hug, a caress, and a few appreciative or encouraging words.

7. Does negative attention act as reinforcement? Give a few examples of negative attention.

Answer: Reinforcement is by definition *anything* that makes a behavior more likely to be repeated. Negative attention—even if painful—can act as reinforcement, with the result that the misbehavior will be repeated. A slap and an angry reprimand are examples of negative attention.

8. What are the four steps to finding and reinforcing the good?

Answer:

- **Ignore the misbehavior.** To lower the frequency of negative behavior, it must not be reinforced; it must be ignored. **Note:** This is true except in a dangerous situation. The teacher needs to spend a little time in a class discussion of what constitutes a dangerous situation.

- **Find behaviors that you feel OK about.** In order to reinforce the behaviors that you want, you must first find those behaviors. It's important to make an effort to find any and all behaviors that you feel OK—or even neutral—about.

- **Reinforce that behavior with positive attention.** Behavior that is reinforced is more likely to be repeated than behavior that is ignored. With both children and adults attention is the most consistent reinforcement. Positive attention is given with a warm smile, a hug, a wink, a caress, an appreciative comment, etc.

- **Gradually start reinforcing only those behaviors you want repeated.** Once the percentage of OK behaviors has increased, you can start being more choosy about what you want to reinforce.

9. How do the parent and the child benefit from finding and reinforcing good behavior?

Answer: The parent-child relationship is improved. Reinforcement makes people feel good and increases their desire to please each other. It's a lot more effective than criticism and is a lot healthier for self-esteem.

Resources

- *The Mola Coloring Book: Images from Molas by the Kuna Indians of the San Blas Islands of Panama.* 1994. Prudence Heffron and Dana Musick. The Mola Collection, Santa Fe/Dallas. 1-800-239-4128 or 1-800-322-4037, ISBN 1-885753-00-4. This book has simple line drawings that can help your students understand how to construct a mola. There are bright pictures of each mola design on the back cover.

Teaching Strategies

❤ Assign chapter 2 reading (*Easy*)

Quickies and Openers

❤ Ten-Minute Free Write (*Easy*)

Purpose: To raise an emotional response (affect) about criticism and positive reinforcement.

Instructions: Pass out notebook paper.
On the first day, ask students to write for ten minutes about a time they were criticized for something they did.

- When was it?

- What happened?

- Who criticized you?

- Why did they criticize you?

- How did you feel after the incident?

On the second day, ask students to write for ten minutes about a time they were given positive attention for something they had done.

- When was it?

- What happened?

- Who gave you the positive attention?

- Why did they give you positive attention?

- How did you feel after the incident?

Debrief after the second day. Ask students to *discuss the difference in the way they felt after each encounter.* Take a vote to find out which one they would rather experience on a regular basis.

Graffiti Wall (*Easy*)

Purpose: To raise awareness that criticism is often used in an attempt to get someone to change their behavior.

Instructions: Put up a huge piece of butcher paper or have students write on the chalkboard. At the top, write the title "Daily Criticisms—Things People Say in Their Attempts to Handle Misbehavior."

Ask students to write criticisms they have heard someone say in an attempt to get a child to change his or her behavior. You might get them started by writing an example: "Stop whining!" or "You sound just like a baby."

Debrief: After you have filled the paper with criticisms, ask the students their opinion of the effectiveness of these kinds of statements. Ask, "What might be some less desirable outcomes of using criticism to correct misbehavior?"

 ## Talk Behind Your Back (*Easy*)

Purpose: To show that positive reinforcement is easy to give and that it makes people feel good about themselves.

Instructions: Ask a volunteer to sit on a chair with his or her back to the class. Then, the teacher and class members talk positively about the volunteer. Ask the class to focus on giving attention to the volunteer's characteristic speech and behavior, rather than to his or her appearance. Emphasize the goal to speak only positive remarks.

Debrief immediately by helping the volunteer discuss how he or she felt while receiving the reinforcing comments.

Sign Behind Your Back (*Easy*)

Purpose: To show that positive reinforcement is easy to give and that it makes people feel good.

Instructions: Supply masking tape and pass out a piece of unruled 8½" x 11" paper to each student.

Ask students to write their names on the top of their papers and then to help each other tape the piece of paper on their backs. Students go around the room writing positive statements on each other's backs. Ask the students to write positive remarks about the person's speech and behavior, rather than on looks or dress.

Debrief by allowing students time to read their own sheets of remarks. Ask how they felt after reading their sheet of positive reinforcement. Ask if it was easy or difficult to come up with positive remarks. You might want to ask if students think it is easier to find and name the positive behavior of a person they know and love or that of an acquaintance.

The Name Game (*Easy*)

Purpose: To allow students to give positive attention to their own behavior.

Instructions: Pass out blank paper.

Ask students to write the letters of their first and last names downward on the left side of the paper. Then, for each letter, they will write a word that describes their best behaviors, a word which begins with that letter. They may have access to a dictionary or thesaurus if one is needed.

Students may need some encouragement to embark on self-praise. After all, one of the greatest fears of adolescence is being seen as "stuck on yourself." You may need to discuss the value and virtue of self-understanding and that it is OK to be able to articulate your positive behaviors.

Example:

C (clever)   S (sweet)

O (organized)   M (merry)

N (nice)   I (inquisitive)

N (natural)   T (truthful)

I (imaginative)   H (happy)

E (eager)

Debrief: Students may be hesitant to share their lists. You may need to repeat the discussion of *the value and virtue of self-understanding and that it is OK to be able to articulate your positive behaviors.* These should definitely be posted around the classroom. Let's be proud of the positive behaviors that we work so hard to develop and practice!

Knowledge

 ## Notetaking (*Easy*)

Purpose: After or during the chapter reading, this will help students organize information about finding and reinforcing the good behavior.

Instructions: Review the notetaking technique explained on **Handout 2**. Use **Overhead 4** to demonstrate how to take notes.

OR

Essential Questions (*Easy*)

Purpose: After or during the chapter reading, this will help students organize information about finding and reinforcing the good behavior.

Instructions: Use **Handout 12**.

OR

 ## Flash Cards (*Easy*)

Purpose: Students recall and organize information about finding and reinforcing the good behavior.

Instructions: Pass out a dozen 3″ x 5″ index cards to each student. Use **Overhead 6** to give instructions.

Give the class time for students to pair up and practice answering flash card questions. Remind them to allow the other student time to think of the answer. Students may refer to their own flash cards for answers. Encourage students to be supportive of each other, by giving hints, prompting, etc. This allows them to discuss chapter concepts. Such discussions increase exposure to and understanding of the concepts.

CAASE Work

 ## Advice Column (*Challenging*)

Purpose: The students show understanding of the chapter contents by "putting them into their own words."

Instructions: Begin by reading one or two examples of advice columns, perhaps one from a major newspaper and one from a teen magazine. Use **Handout 13**. Encourage students to use humor. This may be a great homework assignment.

Debrief: After all responses are written, ask for pairs who are willing to read their letters and advice column responses.

 ## Five-Day Diary (*Average*)

Purpose: Students recognize the role that reinforcement plays in their lives. Students understand the effect of their speech and behavior on the well-being of others.

Instructions: Use **Handout 14**. **Note:** Begin this assignment on the first day you begin study of chapter 2.

Debrief: At the end of five days, discuss findings. Was there enough room on the diary handout? Discuss the frequency of reinforcement in everyday life. Who uses reinforcement? When? Why is it used? Where is it used most often? Ask students if they reinforce their friends. Discuss the types of reinforcement used—positive attention vs. criticism. Discuss the effects of using criticism and positive attention. Did this assignment cause you to give more positive attention to others than you normally do?

❤ Instruction Pamphlet (*Average*)

Purpose: To put concepts together to form instructions for finding and reinforcing good behavior.

Instructions: Use **Handout 15**. Encourage students to produce a quality **Portfolio Piece**. This pamphlet can be copied and used for peer/community education or it might serve as a reminder in the future. Note to teacher: **Handout 17** contains the assessment Rubric for **Handout 15**.

Supply students with 12″ x 18″ white construction paper OR white butcher paper which will be folded to form a pamphlet. Encourage students to use a computer for word processing and line graphics. Supply construction paper in bright colors and black and white, cut into 9″ x 12″ rectangles, for the cover design. You will also need to supply scissors and glue.

Handout 15 instructs students to do a mola design on the cover of their pamphlet. You will need to explain what a mola is.

Molas are fabric ornaments made for clothing by the Kuna Indians of the San Blas Islands of Panama. Molas are made by layering several different colored fabrics, then, cutting through the layers with scissors to make the design, turning the edges under and handstitching them together. Sometimes details are embroidered on top. Traditionally, the mola designs of the Kunas were inspired by their colorful natural surroundings.

❤ Persuasive Speech (*Challenging*)

Purpose: Students justify and convince others that positive reinforcement is more effective than negative attention or criticism.

Instructions: Use **Handouts 16** and **17**.

A copy of the student's speech should go with their instruction pamphlet in **The Portfolio** which students will be compiling throughout the course.

Debrief: You may want to ask volunteers to give their speeches to the class. Discuss the use of positive reinforcement (attention) as a skill needed for all types of relationships and in many situations encountered in everyday life.

Introduction to Chapters
Three and Four

Chapters 3 and 4 assert the importance of interpersonal communication skills in building healthy relationships. It would be helpful to provide an overview of the components of interpersonal communication before assigning these chapters. Here are some suggestions.

"Communication Is" Poster (*Easy*)

Purpose: To provide an overview of the components of interpersonal communication and identify its importance in building relationships.

Instructions: Write the following on a huge piece of butcher paper. Be sure to leave lots of space for students to write their answers.

COMMUNICATION IS ...

1. **SENDING MESSAGES**   *How do we send messages?*

2. **RECEIVING MESSAGES**   *In what ways do we receive messages?*

3. **UNDERSTANDING**   *What do we do to make sure we understand what is being communicated to us?*

Hold an all-class brainstorming session to fill in the ways we send messages, receive messages, and achieve understanding. Here are some answers:

The Ways We Send Messages

- Writing

- Talking

- Body language

The Ways We Receive Messages

- Reading

- Listening

The Ways We Achieve Understanding

Note: Your students may not be able to fill in this section until after they have studied chapter 3. You could allow them to make good guesses or you could just leave it blank for now, and return to fill it out after the chapter 3 reading.

- Asking clarifying questions

- Paraphrasing

- Giving feedback

Debrief: Make the point that communication is *learned* and we all need to practice to improve our skill at it. Introduce the main topics of chapters 3 and 4: listening for understanding and for expressing yourself. Emphasize that communication skills are critical to relationships, especially the parent-child relationship, where the parent is responsible for using healthy communication to nurture and teach.

Leave this poster up in the classroom at least until the class has finished studying chapter 5.

Chapter Three

Listening

Goal

In this chapter you will learn to appreciate the importance of listening attentively as a fundamental building block of good relationships. You will learn the three rules to better listening.

You will also understand how important it is for people to know that someone is listening to them.

Objectives

At the end of this lesson you will

- Identify listening as a fundamental relationship skill

- Know the difference between pseudo listening and real listening

- Be aware that not listening may damage a relationship

- Understand how listening builds trust and respect between people, and self-esteem in individuals

- Know the ten roadblocks to listening and make an effort to avoid them

- Know and practice the three steps to good listening

- Recognize that listening is a learned skill and that we learn it first from role models, and later as a result of much practice

Rationale

Real listening is much more difficult—and more rare—than most people realize. It is one of the most important elements in any good relationship. We can all benefit from learning about and practicing real listening. When you practice good listening, you show others that you respect them. This builds trust in the relationship and bolsters others' self-esteem. This lesson will allow everyone the opportunity to experience really listening and really being heard.

Essential Questions and Answers

1. Why is listening an important relationship skill?

   Answer: Real listening conveys that you want to understand what the other person is saying, thinking, feeling, and needing. Listening enables you to support and help others. People must be heard, understood, and acknowledged in order to get their needs met. Listening is a way to respect others. Receiving respect and support bolsters self-esteem. These interactions strengthen relationships.

2. What is the difference between pseudo listening and real listening?

   Answer: Real listening implies that you want to understand what the other person is saying, thinking, feeling, and needing. It means putting aside your own ideas and judgments about the other person long enough to really hear him or her. Pseudo listening happens when the listener's intention is to "pass" as listening instead of really listening. Pseudo listening occurs when we allow "blocks" to prevent us from really listening.

3. When someone is pseudo listening, what is blocking the listener's ability to really listen?

   Answer: The following behaviors cause pseudo listening and are blocks to real listening:

   - **Mind reading** is paying more attention to what you think the person "really means" instead of paying attention to what he or she is actually saying.

   - **Rehearsing** involves thinking about and planning what you're going to say next instead of really listening to what the other person is saying.

   - **Filtering** involves tuning out certain topics, and hearing only what you want to hear.

- **Judging** means that you've decided ahead of time that the other person is foolish or bad and, therefore, you don't have to really listen, except for evidence to confirm your judgment.

- **Daydreaming** occurs when you're giving only half of your attention to the person speaking, while, internally, your private thoughts are wandering in completely different directions.

- **Advising** occurs when the other person has barely stopped talking before you jump in with advice about the perfect solution, even though "fixing" things may not be what the other person wants.

- **Sparring** involves listening only enough to find something to disagree with, and then defending your position regardless of what the other person says. This includes sarcasm and put-downs.

- **Being right** means that you'll go to any lengths to avoid the suggestion that you're wrong, including lying, shouting, twisting the facts, changing the subject, justifying, making excuses, accusing, etc.

- **Derailing** occurs when you change the subject or laugh it off whenever you become bored or uncomfortable with the conversation.

- **Placating** takes place when you're so concerned with being nice, agreeable, and liked that you agree with everything that is being said without really listening.

4. What might be some outcomes of not listening to children and others?

   Answer:

   - Frustration
   - Needs are not met
   - Causes problems in the relationship
   - Children do not learn from role models how to be a good listener
   - People don't understand each other
   - Lack of trust in the relationship
   - Low self-esteem

5. What are the three rules that promote good listening?

   Answer:

   - Listen with your full attention instead of half listening. Maintain eye contact, nod, lean slightly forward, smile, or frown in sympathy with what is being said.

   - Attend to the feelings as well as to the content of the message. Try to use empathy, which is the ability to put yourself in the other person's shoes and know what that person is feeling. Ask for clarification and more information, in order to understand and acknowledge what the other person is saying.

- Actively acknowledge that you've heard what was said. Use paraphrasing, which means to say in your own words what you've heard the other person say. Give feedback. Tell the person your reaction to what he or she said. Your feedback should be immediate, honest, and supportive.

6. How do individuals benefit and relationships improve when there is *real* listening?

Answer:

- Real listening builds and strengthens relationships

- People get their needs met

- People understand each other (thoughts, feelings, and needs)

- Real listening fosters self-esteem

- It feels good to be heard, understood, and acknowledged

- Real listening builds trust

- Real listening allows people to take risks in relationships

Resources

- Software: Call Educational Resources at (800) 624-2926 for their catalog.

- Software: Call CDL Software Shop at (800) 637-0047 for their catalog.

- Assign chapter 3 reading (Easy)

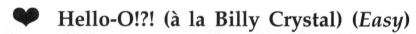

Teaching Strategies

 Assign chapter 3 reading (*Easy*)

Quickies and Openers

Hello-O!?! (à la Billy Crystal) (*Easy*)

Purpose: To raise awareness that everyone needs to know that others care for and listen to them.

Instructions: Divide the class into groups of five or six. Each group sits in a circle.

Ask one person from each group to volunteer to give a quick summary of his or her life to their group. Tell the volunteer speakers that you will give them an outline of events from birth to the present for them to cover (use **Handout 18**).

Explain that the remaining group members will be "listeners." Don't let the speaker know about the instructions to the listeners. (Send all the speakers out of the room for a few moments while you give instructions and pass out the listener instruction cards.) Pass out one instruction card from **Handout 18** to each listener in all groups. Explain that they are to do as instructed on the card. Don't let the volunteer speaker know what is on the listener cards.

Start a timer (set at five minutes) and instruct the speakers to continue their life story, no matter what happens, until they hear it ring. The speaker tells his or her life story, the listeners listen for the first forty seconds and then allow themselves to be distracted as instructed on their cards. After five painful minutes, stop and debrief.

Debrief: Ask the speakers what they saw their listeners doing. Ask the speakers to describe how they *felt* while they were speaking. Discuss the importance of really listening and being listened to.

❤ No Questions Asked! (*Easy*)

Purpose: To demonstrate the importance of asking questions and using both paraphrasing and feedback to achieve active listening.

Instructions: Everyone must have a pencil. Pass out one piece of blank 8½" x 11" paper to each student. Instruct students to fold their papers in half:

Have a paper copy and a transparency copy of **Overhead 7**. Cut the paper copy in half so that each picture is on a separate piece of paper. Do not show these pictures to anyone except to the volunteer who will verbally describe how to draw the picture to the other students.

Round 1

Ask for two volunteers from the class. Explain that each volunteer will describe a picture for the class to draw.

Position a volunteer in a chair or at the podium in front of the classroom. Give them the paper copy of their half of Overhead 7. Tell the whole class that this volunteer will describe picture No. 1 for the class to draw. Out loud, instruct the volunteer to speak clearly and slowly to give the students plenty of time to draw. Volunteers can repeat an instruction if they choose to, but it is not necessary to do so.

Clearly state to the class the following: *No One May Speak Except for The Volunteer. No Questions May Be Asked and Instructions May Not Be Repeated. This Is One-Way Communication!*

After the volunteer has finished describing the picture to the class, project Overhead 7 to show what picture No. 1 should look like. *Keep Picture No. 2 Covered!* Ask students to show their pictures.

Debrief: Laugh and discuss—Why don't the pictures look like the one described? What would enable the listeners to be able to draw a more accurate picture? (Answer: Being able to ask clarifying questions, to paraphrase, and to give feedback.) How did it feel to follow instructions without being able to clarify?

Round 2

Last, have the second volunteer come up to describe picture No. 2. *This Time, Class Members May Ask Clarifying Questions, Paraphrase, or Give Feedback.*

Put up Overhead 7 to show what picture No. 2 should look like. Ask students to show their pictures.

Debrief: Are the pictures more similar to the one described? What made the difference? How did it feel to be able to ask questions, compared to not being able to ask? What does this have to do with everyday listening?

Answer: We need to ask clarifying questions, paraphrase, and give feedback if we want to really listen to others.

♥ No Pseudo Allowed (*Easy*)

Purpose: To make students aware of the focus and concentration required for real listening. This activity does not allow anyone to be a passive listener.

Instructions: Get the whole class to stand in a circle (split the class into two or three circles if you want this activity to take less time). You will need to guide and monitor each circle.

Starting with the person wearing the most purple and moving clockwise, have each person say his or her first name and an activity that they enjoy and would like to be known for. For example: "My name is Piggy and I am a Star." (If Miss Piggy was in your class she would, of course, go first because she would be wearing the most purple.) Or "My name is Dan and I play street hockey."

The next person in the clockwise direction should repeat what the last person said, "Piggy is a Star," and then add his or her own name and interest. "My name is Tony and I play the piano."

The third person says, "Piggy is a star, Tony plays the piano . . . my name is Josh and I do magic." The fourth person would say, "Piggy is a star, Tony plays the piano, Josh does magic . . . my name is _____," and so on, until you have gone all the way around the circle.

Encourage everyone to be patient and *give people a little time to remember and recite* (about 25 seconds); however, also encourage students to prompt anyone who is struggling to remember names and interests. Promote the caring and support of a team attitude. When you teach students the value of being their "brother's keeper," you are giving them a valuable relationship skill that will help them at home and on the job.

Continue until all members of each circle have been introduced.

Debrief: Ask how it felt to be an active listener in this activity. Discuss the level of focus and concentration that was required to perform real listening. Ask students to remember times in their lives when they have really listened to a friend.

Knowledge

❤ Notetaking (*Easy*)

Purpose: After or during chapter reading, this will help students organize information about listening.

Instructions: Review the notetaking technique explained on **Handout 2**. Use **Overhead 4** to demonstrate how to take notes.

OR

❤ Mind Map (*Easy*)

Purpose: This is another method of notetaking. After or during chapter reading, students map out the chapter concepts so that related ideas are grouped together. This creates a visual aid that may help students organize and internalize the information about listening.

Instructions: Students use **Handout 19**. Use **Overhead 8** to get them started on their mind map.

Optional idea for students to create a reminder for future reference: Have students make an actual mobile like the one presented on the mind-map Handout. The basic design issue with a mobile is that it must be balanced. Students could use various colors of poster board stapled or taped to wire clothing hangers, and string to connect the hanging pieces of board. They could write on both sides of the mobile pieces. This could be done as homework. Hang mobiles around the classroom, in the administration building, in the library, and so forth.

OR

❤ Essential Questions (*Easy*)

Purpose: After or during chapter reading, this will help students organize information about listening.

Instructions: Use **Handout 20**.

CAASE Work

❤ Listening Crossword (*Average*)

Purpose: Students practice their understanding of chapter concepts by completing a crossword puzzle.

Instructions: Use **Handout 21**. Most students know how to fill in a crossword puzzle. Be prepared to help individuals who are not able to self-start. Answers are on page 3 of Handout 21.

Another way that you can do this activity: If you have access to crossword puzzle software, such as *Puzzle Power* by Centron, your students may use the software to write their own clues and create their own puzzle from the list of words you assign (use the words from Overhead 12).

❤ Listening Pie (*Average*)

Purpose: Students are made aware of listening as a critical relationship skill when they record the amount of time they spend listening in one day.

Instructions: Students use **Handout 22** to record the amount of time they spend listening in a typical twenty-four-hour "school day" (give this assignment on Monday through Thursday, not on a Friday). Have students begin immediately after you pass out Handout 22. You may make an overhead of the handout to show them how to shade in the time slots. It would be nice if you could borrow clipboards from the track coach (. . . or whoever has thirty clipboards . . .) so that students can carry their record sheets on clipboards to facilitate the constant recording that will be necessary.

Students use **Handout 23** to make a pie chart showing the amount of time they spend in activities that require listening, in activities that do not require listening, and the amount of time spent sleeping in a typical day. **Note:** You will need to provide protractors for making the pie charts.

Debrief: Common sense alone tells us that we spend a lot of time listening throughout the day. With this activity, we're trying to drive home the point that we all need to be skillful listeners because we rely on listening to relate to others and to learn from others. Probably the most telling aspect of the students' pie charts is going to be the overlay of cross-hatching showing the time spent in *real listening* compared to pseudo listening.

Peanut Butter and Jelly (*Average*)

Purpose: This hilarious activity provides an easy and nonthreatening way to compare and contrast pseudo listening and *real* listening. By eliminating parts of the *real* listening process you expose their importance, and students discover the interdependence of verbal expression and *real* listening.

Instructions: Please read *all* of the instructions to this activity in advance.

Make copies of the four motivation/instruction cards (on the following pages) and **Handouts 24, 25, 26,** and **27** in advance. You may laminate these for durability.

Have the following items on a table when the class enters.

Cutting board

Dinner knife or spreading knife

Jar of peanut butter

Jar of jelly

Loaf of bread left in the wrapper

Enough 3" x 5" index cards for the entire class

As soon as the class enters, ask the students to "Please raise your hand if you know how to make a peanut butter and jelly sandwich." Lots of hands should go up. Then, pass out the 3" x 5" index cards and point to the ingredients, explaining that they will make a peanut butter and jelly sandwich today. Ask everyone to write complete instructions on the cards for making a peanut butter and jelly sandwich. Collect the cards.

Ask for two volunteers, one to be a sandwich maker and one to read instructions to the sandwich maker. Seat the sandwich maker at a table facing the class with the first five items listed above in front of him or her on the tabletop. Seat the reader facing away from the class, behind the sandwich maker, almost back to back.

Explain that the goal of this activity is to differentiate between pseudo listening and *real* listening and show that practicing the three rules of *real* listening is the way to achieve effective communication and build relationships. Also, remind the class that *real* listening is practiced by people who *want to understand* what the other person is saying, thinking, feeling, and needing. If the listener does not have that intention, he or she is likely to fall into pseudo listening. You may want to write these two points on the chalkboard in advance.

Round 1

Pick any one of the 3" x 5" cards from the class and give it to the reader.

Give each volunteer the appropriate motivation card and read the cards out loud to the class:

Round 1: Reader Motivation/Instructions

You have no idea how to make a peanut butter and jelly sandwich; however, you desperately need to eat one! You must rely on the sandwich maker to make one for you. Oops! The sandwich maker doesn't know how to make one either! You found a recipe and now you must convey these instructions even though you're not completely sure what the outcome will be. Read the instructions verbatim off the card. You may not communicate with the sandwich maker in any other way. Be a bit dramatic, your voice should have a desperate tone.

Round 1: Sandwich Maker Motivation/Instructions

You have no idea about the reader's problem. You do not know how the reader feels or what the reader needs and, besides, you don't really care. You're trying to do your job as a sandwich maker; however, you don't know how to make a peanut butter and jelly sandwich. You make the sandwich as best you can following the instructions exactly as read. You may not communicate with the reader in any other way. You follow the instructions, but your lack of interest causes you to *Filter out* (skip) one step.

Remind the rest of the class that they may not communicate with the volunteers. The reader begins and the sandwich maker actually tries to make a sandwich. Round 1 of the activity is over when all the instructions have been read once. I've had all kinds of weird and funny outcomes. It really doesn't matter how the sandwich turns out, you'll still have made your point.

Debrief: You might begin by saying, "This was only a sandwich!" Imagine how difficult it is to express yourself or really listen in a real-life situation at home or at work! You might ask some of the following questions to draw some conclusions from Round 1 of the activity:

- What was the outcome of this activity?

- Why? What blocked the sandwich maker's listening and ability to properly make the sandwich?

Answers may include: lack of empathy, filtering, lack of intent to be a *real* listener, and lack of understanding.

- What aspects of effective communication were missing?

Answers must include: asking clarifying questions, empathy, paraphrasing, and feedback.

- How do you think the reader felt during this activity? Did the reader get his or her needs met?

- How do you think the sandwich maker felt during the process? How do you think he or she feels now with this product?

- Would this kind of talking and listening be more likely to solve problems or cause problems in a relationship?

- Did trust build between the two interactors?

Round 2

You may use the same two volunteers or pick two new ones. Draw a different 3" x 5" card from the stack. Have the volunteer sandwich maker sit the same way facing the class with the items in front of him or her on the table. *Have the reader sit across the table, facing the sandwich maker.*

For Round 2, bring up four additional volunteers. Ask them to stand quietly behind the sandwich maker. These players will be your listening experts and will identify *empathy, clarification, paraphrasing,* and *feedback* whenever they become evident in the communication between the reader and the sandwich maker. Give each of these players a different card to hold up. Allow them a few minutes to read the descriptions on side 2 of their cards to become "experts" on their topic. Use **Handouts 24, 25, 26,** and **27**.

Give each volunteer the appropriate motivation card and tell them to read the cards out loud to the class:

Round 2: Reader Motivation/Instructions

You have no idea how to make a peanut butter and jelly sandwich; however, you desperately need to eat one. You must rely on the sandwich maker to make one for you. Oops! The sandwich maker doesn't know how to make one either! You found a recipe and now you must convey these instructions even though you're not completely sure what the outcome will be. *Read the instructions exactly as they appear on the card.* You may communicate with the sandwich maker in any manner to discuss and jointly decide how to make the sandwich properly. **You may add to and clarify the instructions only through discussion with the sandwich maker.** This is the only way you're going to get what you need.

Round 2: Sandwich Maker Motivation/Instructions

You're trying to do your job as a sandwich maker and you *want to understand* what the reader is saying, thinking, feeling, and needing. You do not know how to make a peanut butter and jelly sandwich. As the reader gives instructions, you may communicate with the reader to clarify the instructions. You may ask clarifying questions, you can paraphrase, give feedback, discuss and make joint decisions, etc.

Remind the rest of the class that they may not communicate with the volunteers. The reader begins and the sandwich maker actually makes a sandwich. This time they will probably have a successful outcome.

Debrief: You might ask some of the following questions to focus on the differences between pseudo and real listening:

- In Round 2, what was different about the communication between the reader and the sandwich maker?

- Specifically, what improved the sandwich maker's listening and ability to properly make the sandwich?

Answers may include: empathy, intent to really listen, eye contact, true understanding achieved by asking clarifying questions, paraphrasing, and feedback. **Make the point that these behaviors must be practiced to perform *real* listening.**

- How do you think the reader felt during this activity? Did the reader get his or her needs met?

You might add: Frequently, people struggle to find the right words to effectively communicate their needs and feelings. A skilled listener can facilitate understanding.

- How do you think the sandwich maker felt during the process and now with his or her product?

- Would this kind of listening be more likely to solve problems or cause problems in a relationship?

- Did trust build between the two interactors?

Close the debriefing by emphasizing that *effective self-expression on the part of one person and real listening on the part of another person work together to create good communication.*

Listening Questionnaire (*Challenging*)

Purpose: Students develop a questionnaire to raise awareness about pseudo listening versus *real* listening. The students' depth of understanding of the practice of listening will be highly challenged as they must develop an assessment tool—the **Portfolio Piece.**

Instructions: Students use **Handout 28** to develop their questionnaire and rating scale.

The teacher must provide several examples of questionnaires from magazines. Copy them onto overhead transparencies to: 1) show how they are worded to examine the reader's knowledge of the topic, 2) show how the scoring system is used, and 3) show how the scoring profiles are written.

Students should make four copies of their questionnaire: one is turned in blank, one is administered to a friend, one is administered to one of their parents, and the other is self-administered to rate their own listening skills. The completed and scored questionnaires are also turned in to the teacher.

Chapter Four

Expressing Yourself

Goal

In this chapter you will learn the rules of expressing yourself in the most useful and healthy way and will have the opportunity to practice those rules.

Objectives

At the end of this lesson you will

- Understand that when we express ourselves we are giving information about ourselves (i.e., our needs, wants, feelings, etc.)

- Understand that the best way to receive cooperation from another person is by expressing ourselves appropriately

- Know and understand the rules for healthy expression

- Have the experience of being on the giving and receiving end of both healthy expression and unhealthy expression

Rationale

All people express themselves all the time; it's how we get our needs met and it's the way we convey our likes, dislikes, thoughts, feelings, wants, opinions, reactions, and decisions. It is our way of getting cooperation from others and it is how we initiate changes in the speech and behavior of others. Appropriate expression is more likely to be heard and to engage the cooperation of others. Expressing yourself effectively is one of the most important elements in any good relationship.

Essential Questions and Answers

1. Why is it important to express yourself?

    Answer: Self-expression is everything one says and does. It is the way we get our needs met and it is the way we convey likes, dislikes, thoughts, feelings, wants, opinions, reactions, and decisions to others. It's the way we get others to cooperate with us.

2. What are the three steps in expressing yourself?

    Answer:

    (1) Describe the situation. First, describe the situation; then say why the situation is a problem for you.

    (2) Use an "I" statement to describe your feelings. This is a way of taking responsibility for your feelings instead of blaming the other person with a "you" statement. Begin by saying, "I feel . . . ," and continue by filling in the way you feel about the situation. An "I" statement is more likely to be heard.

    (3) Describe what you want or need in the situation. Be clear about what it is that you want or need in the situation.

3. What are some tips for better self-expression?

    Answer:

    Be clear: Clearly state your thoughts, feelings, wants, and needs, without leaving anything out or beating around the bush.

    Be honest: State your true feelings and needs without fear of upsetting the other person. Lies keep you cut off from others and unable to express yourself.

    Be consistent: Your posture, tone of voice, and gestures should match the content of what you're saying. Sometimes, incongruities between verbal and nonverbal messages indicate that you don't really know how you feel. You may need to check inside yourself to make sure how you are really feeling.

    Be immediate: Quickly telling someone how you feel, especially children, gives them the opportunity to adjust their behavior. Waiting may diminish the value of your feedback.

Be supportive: Remember that your intention in expressing yourself is to be heard and understood, not to hurt the other person or to prove yourself right.

Be appropriate: The expression of your feelings needs to match the strength of those feelings. Violent behaviors and words are never appropriate.

4. What are some communication habits that interfere with self-expression and should be avoided?

Answer:

Judging: "You" statements accuse and attack the other person.

Labeling: Calling names and labeling is a condemnation of the person rather than the behavior.

Lecturing and moralizing: No one likes to be told they're wrong.

Commanding: Commands imply a lack of equality and respect in a relationship and can trigger a refusal to comply.

Threatening: Threats serve no purpose other than to intimidate the other person into behaving the way you want them to. The more fear there is in a relationship, the less room there is for respect and caring.

Making negative comparisons: These contain "you're bad" messages and they make people feel inferior to others. They arouse feelings of defensiveness rather than a desire to understand feelings and needs and to improve the relationship.

Teaching Strategies

 ### Assign chapter 4 reading (*Easy*)

Quickies and Openers

Opener No. 1 stimulates emotional responses to something we take for granted—expressing ourselves. The other openers raise awareness of the "do's" and "don'ts" of expressing yourself.

 ### Hand to Hand (*Easy*)

Purpose: By limiting the students' ability to express themselves, we raise awareness of its importance.

Instructions: In advance, place paper and pencils on a chair and clear enough space around the chair.

This activity can be done by four volunteer pairs (eight students) or the entire class all at once. Have students pair up (with someone with whom they don't mind holding hands) and ask them to stand face-to-face with all the pairs forming a circle around the chair. One person from each pair comes up to the teacher to get *special instructions*. The other partners stay and wait quietly for their partner to return.

Special Instructions: Give each person a secret number (beginning with the number 1). Explain that you have placed pencils and paper on the chair in the center of the circle. With *eyes closed* and *using only their hands* they will ask their partner to get a piece of paper, fold it in half, and write their secret number on it. They must hold up the paper to show that they are done. Emphasize that there must be *no talking* and they must *keep their eyes closed* while they're trying to communicate with their partner.

Out loud: Instruct the numbered partners to return to their places around the chair, hold hands with their partner, and close their eyes. The partners without numbers may keep their eyes open. Explain that the numbered partners will use *only their hands* to ask their partners without numbers to do a task. There is *no talking* during this activity. When all pairs seem to be finished, allow everyone to return to their seats.

Debrief: Ask, "Did you understand what your partner was trying to communicate?" "How did it feel to be limited to communicating with your hands only?" and "How did it feel to try to understand something communicated only with hands?" Finally, you might want to take a quick opinion poll: "Raise your hand if you're glad that we have many ways with which we express ourselves."

I Heard It Through the Grapevine (*Easy*)

Purpose: This opener demonstrates the importance of clear, immediate, and appropriate self-expression.

Instructions: This is the classic activity where the teacher gives one student a message and they whisper it in the ear of the next person, who whispers it to a third person, and so on until the message has been passed on by everyone in the class. The sender may whisper the message only two times. Here's a sample message: "People express themselves all the time." You can also make up your own message. The message can be anything: a complete sentence or a sentence fragment, a book or movie title, and so forth.

Debrief: The message *always* gets garbled! This activity illustrates so many of the "do's" and "don'ts" of communication. Ask, "What was wrong with the way we tried to communicate this message?" Guide discussion around the following three steps for expressing yourself:

1. Speakers need to express themselves clearly.

2. Messages are better understood when they are expressed immediately and directly to one person.

3. The expression must be appropriately delivered.

❤ Identify a Don't (*Average*)

Purpose: During this opener, the students identify the "don'ts" of self-expression.

Instructions: This opener is based on the possible ways someone could inappropriately express himself or herself in the following situation.

Billy works at a neighborhood pizza parlor. When he accepted the job, there was an agreement that all employees would take turns working on Saturdays and everyone would have at least one Saturday off each month. This month, his supervisor scheduled him for the first three Saturdays and he was to have the last Saturday of the month off from work. On Friday, after Billy has already made plans with friends, the supervisor asks him to work all day Saturday to cover a baseball team party.

This situation has repeated itself for the past three months and each time the supervisor pleads desperation due to short staff and last-minute bookings.

Billy is tired of working more than he agreed to, he is angry at his supervisor's lack of planning, and he doesn't want to cancel his other plans. He also worries that the supervisor will become angry with him if he says "No." Billy likes his job and doesn't want to jeopardize his position.

- "If you don't stop asking me to work extra hours I'll just quit!" (**Threatening**)

- "Why can't you be like our last supervisor, she never made mistakes like this!" (**Making negative comparisons**)

- "You're worthless at scheduling! Why should I work extra when you're just too lazy to take the time to make a good schedule!" (**Labeling**)

- "This is your problem, hire some new employees!" (**Giving commands**)

- "You never schedule enough staff and we have to come in at the last minute to cover your mistakes!" (**Judging**)

- "You need to plan ahead next time. So far, you've been lucky, there's always someone who can fill in at the last minute, but someday you're going to be short staffed and you'll pay for it! This isn't fair to any of us." (**Lecturing** and **Moralizing**)

Of course, many teenagers will think these statements are fine just the way they are! That's to be expected as teens are in a stage of life when they're beginning to fine-tune communication skills. Well, that's where we come in; we're teachers and it's our job to present more effective alternatives and help them become more confident of their abilities.

Billy obviously needs to express himself. For the purpose of identifying the "don'ts of expressing yourself," all of the examples of Billy's possible statements to his supervisor are inappropriate.

Read one or two of Billy's possible statements each day (or read all of them in one day) and have your class guess which "don't" is being practiced. **Do not read the bold-faced answers**.

Ask the students, "Do you think Billy will express his feelings or satisfy his needs by expressing himself in this way?" After the class guesses the "don't," they can suggest a more appropriate way for Billy to express himself. This will engage the students in following the three steps for expressing themselves and the six "do's" of self-expression.

You may want to write the six "don'ts" on the chalkboard or a poster, or you can have students refer to their notes. For visual processing, you could write each of these statements on an overhead transparency, leaving space to add student suggestions for more appropriate expressions.

Knowledge

 Make a Mask (*Easy*)

Purpose: Using a mind-mapping mask is a method of notetaking that will help students organize the rules of self-expression. Discuss self-expression. Here's a chance to connect the concepts to visual images, thus enhancing memory and learning.

Instructions: Use **Handout 29**. Get students started by having them write (1) "Expressing Yourself" on the nose, (2) "Three Steps in Expressing Yourself" on the mouth, (3) "Do's" on one eye, and (4) "Don'ts" on the other eye. On the circular outline of the mask, they should write (5) the reasons that explain "Why self-expression is important." Encourage them to fill in the details of each of these five concepts by drawing and writing notes in and outside the spaces.

OR

 Essential Questions (*Easy*)

Purpose: For students to learn the importance of self-expression.

Instructions: Use **Handout 30**.

CAASE Work

❤ Three Step (*Challenging*)

Purpose: Students will demonstrate their understanding of the three steps in self-expression by rewording statements.

Instructions: Use **Handout 31**. This activity will be more effective if the students are encouraged to get ideas straight out of chapter 4 in the student reader.

If you choose to assign this comprehension activity, it could be followed up with the following analysis activity (Diagramming). As you can see, this will allow students to evaluate and correct their own work.

❤ Diagramming (*Challenging*)

Purpose: Students will examine the expressions they wrote on Handout 31 to check that they include the three basic steps of self-expression.

Instructions: Use **Handout 32**.

❤ Feeling Bag (*Average*)

Purpose: Students recall events in their own lives that involved strong feelings. This activity illustrates that some experiences and the feelings they generate are very powerful and can influence the way we express ourselves for years after they occur.

Instructions: Make a copy of the following words, cut the words apart, and place them in a bag:

frightened	disappointed	happy
disgusted	angry	sad
surprised	shy	depressed
confused	terrified	annoyed
guilty	satisfied	successful
overwhelmed	peaceful	secure
rushed	shocked	frustrated
loved	betrayed	supported

Begin by saying that the purpose of this activity is to show that some experiences and the feelings they generate are very powerful and can continue to influence the way we express ourselves long after the experience has passed. This activity also gives everyone some practice in expressing themselves.

Explain that a bag will be passed around, and, one at a time, everyone will pick out a word that describes a feeling. Explain that you would like them to recall a time when they experienced the feeling written on the slip of paper in a very strong way, and that you would like them to tell their story to the class. Ask everyone to agree to keep everything that is said in strict confidence. Students need not tell a story they feel uncomfortable with and may draw a second word from the Feeling Bag if they don't feel comfortable with their first pick. Expect everyone to participate in some way.

Debrief: Obviously, this activity will take time, so debriefing must be quick. It would be effective to ask if two or three people could respond to this question: "Have you noticed that feelings generated by past experiences have influenced the way you express yourself today?"

Imagine (*Challenging*)

Purpose: Students will imagine what their school would be like if everyone was perfectly skilled in expressing themselves.

Instructions: Use **Handout 33**. "Free Write" is like writing a first draft in a creative writing assignment. Explain to your students that they should focus on expressing their ideas rather than on perfect grammar.

Grade Card (*Challenging*)

Purpose: Students will produce a grade card listing the criteria for useful (healthy) self-expression. (**Portfolio Piece**)

Instructions: Students use **Handout 34**.

Chapter Five

Whose Problem Is It?

Goal

In this chapter you will learn how to determine who owns the problem in a situation and which communication skill to apply: listening or expressing yourself.

Objectives

At the end of this lesson you will

- Know how to determine who owns the problem in a variety of situations

- Recognize that being able to determine who owns the problem is a skill that enables you to take responsibility in relationships appropriately, knowing when and how to respond

Rationale

On a daily basis, we encounter "problem" situations that require effective communication skills. Knowing who "owns" the problem is essential to determining how to respond in a particular situation. When you own the problem, you have the responsibility for trying to solve it (possibly by expressing yourself). When the other person owns the problem, your responsibility is to listen and be supportive, allowing the other person to solve his or her own problem and resisting the urge to take over. When you give others the message that you think they are capable of solving their own problems, you will build healthy relationships and make your life easier. Also, you will be respected for taking responsibility in solving your own problems.

Essential Questions and Answers

1. When a problem situation arises, how do you determine who owns the problem?

   Answer: You ask yourself, "Whose rights are being violated?" OR "Whose needs are not being met?"

There are four possible scenarios in response to the question:

   (1) The *other person* owns the problem when his or her needs or rights are being thwarted, not yours. Dealing with the problem or finding a solution is his or her responsibility.

   (2) When the other person is satisfying his or her needs and the behavior isn't interfering with your rights in any way, then there's *no problem*.

   (3) When the other person is satisfying his or her needs but the behavior is interfering with your rights or your needs, then the problem *is yours*. You own the problem and the responsibility for solving the problem is yours.

   (4) When the other person has a problem because her needs or rights are being thwarted, but that person's reactions or attempts to solve the problem are interfering with your needs or rights, then you *both* have a problem.

2. What communication skill would you use when you own the problem?

   Answer: You need to use your skills at expressing yourself with "I" messages.

3. What communication skill would you use when the other person owns the problem?

   Answer: Listening. Active listening is the process of helping another person feel heard and understood.

4. How does the skill of being able to determine who owns the problem benefit both individuals and relationships?

   Answers: When you allow people to solve their own problem, you give them the message that you think they are capable. The use of active listening shows that you care about the other person and that you respect his or her feelings. These practices will build your relationship with that person.

   When you take responsibility for your own problems and resist the urge to take on the problems of others, your life will be easier.

Children need to develop into separate individuals with their own identities in order to become autonomous and independent. Parents can promote this development by allowing children to make their own decisions and deal with their own problems in their own way.

5. Why is it sometimes difficult to "let go" when a problem really isn't your responsibility?

Answer: It's especially hard to "let go" when you feel strongly about an issue or situation. Many parents want some measure of control over their children's lives, and they try to mold their children into conforming with their own beliefs and values.

6. What are some of the drawbacks of taking over someone else's problem?

Answer: Taking over someone else's problem doesn't allow that person the opportunity to solve it. You may also be sending a message that you don't think the person can solve his or her own problems. Fighting over things that aren't your responsibility is not only going to make your life more difficult, it may also jeopardize the relationship with that person.

Note: When introducing this chapter, teachers might need to assess their students' understanding of "rights" and "needs." An understanding of these concepts is necessary before they can analyze who owns the problem. Therefore, I have added two more essential questions about rights and needs. The answers given are not in the student reader; however, they can be used to promote a basic understanding of rights and needs. There is a great overview of rights in chapter 5 of the student reader, and the subject of needs as they relate to nurturing was introduced in chapter 1.

7. What are our basic rights?

Answer: A right is something to which one has a just claim; the power or privilege to which a person or a group is justly entitled.

Note: It is not our right to control or manipulate the behavior of another.

8. What are our basic needs?

Answer: A need is a physiological or psychological requirement necessary for the well-being of an organism (person).

Teaching Strategies

The content of previous chapters was probably already familiar to students and for that reason easier to learn. A teacher could achieve the objectives of those chapters by choosing some or all of the teaching strategies that are offered. The content of chapter 5 is probably not familiar to most young people, therefore, this chapter needs a different teaching approach! I recommend following this entire sequence of teaching strategies.

Opener

♥ Revisiting the "Communication Is . . ." Poster *(Easy)*

Purpose: Completing the "Communication Is . . ." Poster will help students to see how communication skills work to create better interpersonal communication.

Instructions: In the introduction to chapters 3 and 4, your class created a poster overview of communication. Refer back to it now.

1. Review the three main parts of communication and under the heading "Ways We Send Messages," add "'I' Messages" next to "Talking." Remind your class that "I" messages are the most effective way to express yourself. (This was a main point in chapter 4.)

2. Draw a huge circle around the "Understanding" section of the poster with an arrow pointing back up to "Listening." Write "Active Listening" on the arrow, reminding students that they learned in chapter 3 that asking clarifying questions, paraphrasing, and giving feedback are the three most important methods we have to perform effective listening.

3. Then, ask the rhetorical question, "When a problem arises in a relationship, how do you know when to listen and how do you know when to express yourself?" You don't need to get an actual answer; however, you could introduce the chapter 5 reading by stating, "Your response, either listening or expressing yourself, is determined by who owns the problem. Chapter 5 explains how to determine who owns the problem in interpersonal communication. Being able to recognize who owns the problem will help you be a better communicator and a better friend."

♥ Assign chapter 5 reading *(Easy)*

Knowledge

♥ Idea Clouds *(Easy)*

Purpose: This activity is just another way for students to take notes as they read chapter 5. Doing this will help students to locate and organize the chapter's main points.

Instructions: Use **Handout 35**.

Debrief: It might be effective to discuss the main ideas as a class OR to collect the Handouts to check that students included most of the main ideas (see Essential Questions and Answers earlier in this chapter for main ideas).

CAASE Work

Quickie (*Easy*)

Purpose: Now that the students have read chapter 5, this brief activity will allow them to relate the concept "Whose problem is it?" to their everyday lives.

Instructions: Ask, "Have you ever tried to solve a problem that was owned by someone else?" OR "Has someone else ever taken over a problem you owned and should have solved by yourself?" If someone answers "yes" to that question, ask, "What happened?" Hopefully, two or three students will volunteer an example. If no one can think of one, you should be prepared with a personal, real-life example. The purpose here is to tie the theory in the chapter to the fact that determining who owns the problem is a skill we all can use on a daily basis.

❤ Bill of Rights and Needs (*Average*)

Purpose: This activity is meant to create a deeper understanding of the basic rights and needs of people that become issues in relationships. The students were exposed to these concepts when they read chapter 5. An understanding of these concepts is necessary to analyze who owns the problem.

Instructions: Put up one large piece of butcher paper. Allow space for several students to write on the paper at the same time. Place several felt-tip pens nearby.

Write "RIGHTS AND NEEDS" at the top of the paper. Refer to what was presented in chapter 5 as you give a brief introduction to basic human rights and needs, and perhaps even tell a personal story.

Please write the following definitions on the chalkboard:

Need: *A physiological or psychological requirement necessary for the well-being of an organism (person).*

Right: *Something to which one has a just claim; the power or privilege to which a person or a group is justly entitled.*

Ask, "What are our basic needs?" and "What are our basic rights?" Then, ask students to go to a poster and write a need or a right. Encourage everyone to get up and write at least one idea. Play some music and give students about six minutes.

Note: The reason for grouping rights and needs on the same poster and treating them as if they are different words for the same concept is that many of our basic rights and needs are related. For example, safety and security are basic needs and they are also basic rights. By grouping them together, you will avoid splitting hairs over what is a right and what is a need. It is not necessary to distinguish between the two for the purpose of determining who owns the problem.

Debrief: Quickly read each entry, briefly discuss, and determine whether it is a need/right. If an entry doesn't seem to fit the definition of a right or a need draw a circle around it. For example, any form of "getting your own way" is *not* a need or a right! Follow this activity immediately by having students interpret needs/rights by providing some common examples.

After class, copy the list of rights and needs (excluding the circled ones) onto a fresh poster and leave it up during the work on this chapter. You could even copy the list onto aged-looking paper (brown it, burn the edges, water spot it, etc., so that it looks like an old copy of the Bill of Rights) and title it "Bill of Rights and Needs."

❤ Bill of Rights/Needs in Everyday Life (*Average*)

Purpose: To generate real-life examples of rights being violated and needs not being met.

Instructions: Form groups of four students. Give each group a piece of butcher paper (about 36" x 18") and a colored felt-tip pen.

Instruct the groups to title the paper, "Everyday Examples: Violation of Rights or Needs Not Being Met." The groups will brainstorm and write as many as they can think of in four minutes. They can look at the "Bill of Rights and Needs" list that you just completed for ideas. They can discuss some of the examples from chapter 5. They can also provide examples from their daily lives; for example, someone may tell about a secret that was betrayed or a friend who drives carelessly with others in the car.

Debrief: Have each group read at least one of their examples.

❤ Puzzled About Who Owns the Problem? (*Easy*)

Purpose: In this activity, the students complete a diagram to translate the main ideas into a progression of events.

Instructions: Each student gets a copy of **Handout 36**. Note: Because the figures on the second page will have to be cut out, the two pages of **Handout 36** must be copied separately on two separate pieces of paper.

Debrief: Show the properly completed diagram on **Overhead 9**.

❤ Gifts (*Easy*)

Purpose: One meaning of the word "gift" is to provide someone else with some power, quality, or attribute. In this activity the students will make a gift that they hope will provide a friend or relative with the power to determine who owns the problem. The process of making this gift will require students to design a guide containing instructions for determining who owns the problem. They will use their guide in the *E Pluribus Unum* activity at the end of this lesson to decide who owns the problem in one of their daily encounters.

Instructions: The guide will be made in the form of a bookmark. The students will make two bookmarks, one to put in their Portfolio, and one to give to a friend or relative. Use **Handout 37**.

Materials Needed for this project are as follows:

Stiff paper (old file folders)

Single hole punch

Scissors

Glue

A variety of unusual and attractive string, yarn, embroidery thread, etc.

Beads

Scraps of fabric, wrapping paper, art paper, etc.

Glitter? Tinsel? Charms? Wire?

Magazines to cut out tiny pictures?

Clear contact paper for a protective covering, or help the students acquire lamination

❤ E Pluribus Unum (*Average*)

Purpose: Students will apply their understanding of how to determine who owns the problem by reporting on just one of the many times that they encounter this issue in a typical day.

Instructions: Use **Handout 37**.

Have the students turn in their assignments: The bookmark and report must be attached to **Handout 37**. After grading, they will go into the students' Portfolios together.

Chapter Six

Problem Solving

Chapter Overview

Goal

In this chapter you will learn the five-step approach to problem solving.

Objectives

At the end of this lesson you will

- Understand that whenever people get together there will be inevitable conflicts of need, that the needs of all people involved are valid, and that any solution to the problem of different needs must take all needs into account.

- Recognize that a five-step approach can be used in problem solving, decide the situations where it would be appropriate to use the five-step process, and know how to use this process to solve problems.

Rationale

No two people have exactly the same needs. Therefore, whenever people get together there will be inevitable conflicts of need. Different needs do not imply that one person is right and the other wrong. The needs of all people are valid and any solution to the problem of different needs must take both sets of needs into account. Problems can be solved by seeking compromise through the five-step problem-solving process. Using a modified version of this process can be a great way to bring small children into the problem-solving process.

Essential Questions and Answers

1. What causes problems between people?

   Answer: An inevitable conflict of needs.

2. How can problems created by a conflict of needs be solved?

   Answer: Use the five-step approach to problem solving to develop a compromise solution.

3. What are the five steps of the problem-solving process and how are they carried out?

   Answer:

   - **Define the problem in terms of conflicting needs.** If the people involved are defining the problem in different ways, they won't be talking about the same issue and will have trouble reaching a resolution. Also, framing the problem as a conflict of needs prevents blaming.

   - **Brainstorm possible solutions.** It helps the process to brainstorm and write down a list of possible solutions. Judging or criticizing suggestions does not help this process. Adding some humor, however, might help a lot!

   - **Evaluate and eliminate alternatives.** Read each item on the list aloud. Discuss each and cross off the suggestions that either won't work or are unacceptable to anyone.

   - **Pick the best solution and develop a plan.** Develop a detailed plan for putting the solution (or combination of solutions) into effect. Include what each person will do and when. Decide when and how you will evaluate whether the plan is working.

   - **Evaluate.** If the plan is working, partners in the problem-solving process should feel some level of satisfaction. Remember that you reached a compromise, so it's possible that no one will be *completely* satisfied. If the plan is found to be unsuccessful, try to find the cause and develop a new plan.

4. What kind of solution will be the outcome of the five-step problem-solving process?

   Answer: A compromise.

5. What might be some of the pitfalls experienced while going through the five-step problem-solving process?

   Answers:

   - Believing that one person's needs are more important or more right.

   - Individuals defining the problem in different ways.

   - Blaming the other for causing the problem.

   - Not writing down all the suggestions.

   - Judging or criticizing a suggestion.

   - Sometimes, partners decide that it is too much work to follow through with the agreed upon changes.

   - Sometimes, each person will wait for the other to "prove" that he or she is committed before committing themselves.

   - Sometimes, neither partner wants to take responsibility for the compromise—to own it—and, therefore, chooses to feel coerced into a compromise solution.

   - There are times when a solution is unsuccessful simply because circumstances have changed.

Teaching Strategies

Quickie Opener

 Free for All (*Easy*)

Purpose: To stimulate an emotional response about effective and ineffective ways to solve problems. To show that individuals, couples, and groups of people often come together in everyday life to solve problems.

Instructions: Divide the class into groups of four or use existing table groups. Give all groups the same problem and tell them they need to find a solution to the problem. There's no need to tell the class how long they have for this activity. Walk around and listen to group discussions, take note of what is said and the different ways the groups approach the task of problem solving. Stop the activity when all groups have come up with a solution.

Here are two possible problems (prepare enough copies for each group in advance):

For several weeks, the four of you (or five, or six) have been planning an all-day trip to the beach. Everyone is ready to go tomorrow; you have parental permission, you have a car, money, have purchased some food, packed clothes, towels, equipment, etc. Everyone is excited at the prospect of having a great day. On the five o'clock news you hear that there is an 80-percent chance of a rainstorm and people are advised to stay away from the beach. All parents withdraw permission to go to the beach. You all get together immediately to decide what to do about this problem. What's your solution?

You are senior class officers. It is now two weeks before the senior class all-night party. The party was planned to be a fabulous boat cruise with a live band on one deck, a DJ on another deck, food, a magic show, food, a comedy show, more food, and so forth. Everyone has been looking forward to this party because it's the first time that a senior class has ever had an off-campus all-night party. The company that plans these parties calls to inform you that they accidentally booked two parties on the same night. They apologize and explain that there is nothing they can do about it. They will return the deposit and will pay a $500 failure fee as was agreed in the contract. They have no further obligation. You call a meeting to decide what to do about this problem. What's your solution?

Debrief: Ten minutes isn't really enough time to actually handle a complicated problem. The objective of this activity is not to come up with a fantastic solution. *The objective is to examine the process that the groups use (or fail to use) in examining a problem and arriving at a compromise solution.* In my class, groups come up with solutions in about one minute. They never use a process and they generally produce an ineffective solution because they failed to properly define the problem. Ask the groups to report on what happened using the following questions:

- Did they achieve anything? Did they come up with a compromise with which every member could live?

- Was there chaos or an organized approach to finding a solution? Did one person take over or did everyone contribute?

- What process did they use, if any?

- How did group members feel during this activity? Was it frustrating? Was it fun?

Make the point that using a previously agreed-upon process or procedure can make problem solving more effective. Chapter 6 presents a widely accepted five-step problem-solving process that can be used in a variety of settings. Stress the fact that they will encounter the same process being used in the workplace and in their community and that it can be used in the family.

❤ **Assign chapter 6 reading (*Easy*)**

Knowledge

❤ **Japanese Notebook (*Easy*)**

Purpose: Students organize and summarize information they read chapter 6.

Instructions: After students have read chapter 6, use **Handout 38** to make Japanese notebooks and fill in the pages as instructed on the handout. The Japanese notebook becomes part of the students' Portfolios.

Materials Needed:

8½″ x 11″ plain paper (enough for four pieces per student)

8½″ x 14″ plain paper (enough for two pieces per student)

9½″ x 6½″ pieces of thin cardboard (enough for two pieces per student)

String, yarn, raffia, twine, etc. (each student will need a piece 16″ in length)

Each student will need two 8½″ x 11½″ pieces of decorative paper and two 5½″ x 8½″ pieces of the same decorative paper (this can be brought from home; it can be construction paper, gift wrap, butcher paper that students print themselves, or you could even use fabric).

Glue

Rulers

Scissors? Perhaps a paper cutter?

A single hole punch

CAASE Work

❤ Five Steps to Problem Solve vs. Three Steps to Express Yourself (*Average*)

Purpose: Students recognize problem situations that call for the use of self-expression versus the five-step problem-solving process.

Instructions: In advance, make copies of **Handouts 39** and **40**. These can be copied on colored paper; the five pages of Handout 39 should be one color and the three pages of Handout 40 a different color. The pages can be laminated for durability.

Part 1: Ask for eight volunteers. Give each volunteer a card in random order and ask them to stand facing the class. Instruct the five students with Handout 39 cards to decide the order of the five steps of problem solving, then to stand in that order while holding up their cards. Simultaneously, the other three volunteers should hold up the three steps of expressing yourself that are described in Handout 40. Check the order. Be sure that each person reads his or her card in order. After this activity, the cards can be put up on a bulletin board.

Part 2: Students read and complete **Handout 41**. Then, when they have completed answering the questions, pass out page 2 of Handout 41.

Debrief: Allow the situations described in **Handout 41** to stimulate discussion about the different kinds of conflicts that can arise between people and the various ways people approach problem solving. Make the point that the five-step problem-solving process is not appropriate in every situation. A *brief* discussion of each is given in page 2 of Handout 41.

❤ Product Failure (*Challenging*)

Purpose: Students apply the five-step problem-solving process to solve a problem and create something new.

Instructions: Help students pair up. Tell half of the pairs that they are A Teams and tell the other half that they are B Teams. Pass out **Handout 42 for A TEAMS** to the A Teams and **Handout 42 for B TEAMS** to the B Teams. Pair an A Team with a B Team. Emphasize that the A Teams are experts in the five-step problem-solving process and need to use their expertise to guarantee that the process is being applied correctly.

Require *each* student to complete his or her own Handout 42. Instruct students to look back at the summaries they wrote in their Japanese notebooks. These summaries should give details of how to carry out each step of the problem-solving process.

Note: The teacher plays an important role in this activity. Periodically, the teacher needs to check on the progress of each team. You might announce that you are playing the role of Management. The teams will need your insight for each step.

Reality Check: When I did this activity with my class, six out of seven groups wrongly defined and interpreted the problem. Therefore, they were unable to complete the remaining steps of the process effectively. Several groups came up with what they thought was a dandy solution in about three minutes! That was a dead giveaway that they had not done the process correctly.

Recommendations: This would be a great activity to invite five or six of your School to Career business partners to play the role of Management (teacher) one for each group. Of course, you should give them a little preparation in advance:

For Step 1: The problem must be correctly defined and must appear in the same language on each team member's paper.

For Step 2: Go over the rules of brainstorming. Every idea must be listened to and written down, no matter how far out it sounds. It may end up being a great idea when altered or teamed with another lame idea. Try to fill in all of the lines on the Handout.

For Step 3: This step should involve much time in discussion of the alternatives. The teacher (Management) can allow the teams to commit a small expenditure of money as part of the solution, but, remember, the company is already in the red for the materials used to make the play dough.

For Step 4: The solution can be any compromise that everyone agrees is somewhat realistic and will work. Look for a sound plan of action.

❤ Broadcast Journalist (*Challenging*)

Purpose: The students will write and report on the newsworthy aspects of the five-step problem-solving process.

Instructions: Use **Handout 43**. Encourage students to listen to the TV news to get some ideas about how a feature story is delivered. Encourage students to videotape themselves for extra credit. This is fun to do with friends.

Set up a news desk (like the ones the anchors sit behind on TV) in your classroom and have students come up one at a time to deliver their reports. If students hand in a videotape, you can show the tapes instead of staging a live delivery.

Chapter Seven

Choices and Consequences

Goal

In this chapter you will learn how offering choices and allowing people to experience the consequences of their behavior molds and encourages self-esteem and responsible behavior in children (and others).

Objectives

At the end of this lesson you will

- Understand why punishment is not an effective response to misbehavior

- Understand that offering choices builds a child's (or anyone's) self-esteem and that experiencing consequences builds responsibility

- Be able to tell the difference between natural and logical consequences

- Be able to develop appropriate choices and consequences for a variety of situations.

Rationale

A parent's ultimate goal is to produce a mature, responsible adult. To achieve this goal parents are called upon to build a child's self-esteem while setting appropriate limits. Punishment does not achieve either of these goals for many reasons. Parents will be more effective nurturers if they offer choices and allow children to experience the consequences of their behavior.

When children are given choices, they learn that they have the power to make decisions for themselves. They learn that they can make good decisions or bad decisions, and that their choices will bring consequences. Without these choices, children would never be able to learn how to behave in the most responsible ways.

Essential Questions and Answers

1. Why is punishment an ineffective response to misbehavior?

   Answers:

   - Punishment almost always involves anger. Instead of teaching responsibility, you are teaching your child to be afraid of you.

   - Punishment teaches children to do what you want them to do to avoid the punishment rather than because it's the right thing to do. Instead of teaching children how to make better, more responsible decisions, you are teaching them that it is better to be sneaky than to be caught misbehaving.

   - Punishment is often unrelated to the misbehavior. Children can't learn why their behavior was wrong or how to make more responsible decisions based on anticipated consequences.

   - Punishment sometimes makes children so angry that, instead of thinking about how to behave more appropriately, they are distracted with revenge fantasies.

   - Physical punishment teaches that "might makes right," that you can get what you want through the use of power and coercion.

   - Sometimes punishment provides some much desired attention and by doing so actually can reinforce the misbehavior.

2. How does giving children choices and allowing them to experience consequences contribute to self-esteem and responsibility?

   Answer: When children are given choices, they learn that they have the power to make decisions for themselves. They learn that they can make good decisions or bad decisions, and that their choices will bring consequences. Without these choices, children would never be able to learn how to behave in the most responsible ways. These experiences help the child to develop independence and self-esteem. Giving choices separates the do-er from the deed. It is a way of letting the child know that you don't like the behavior without condemning the child as bad. Giving choices and allowing a child to experience consequences fosters an honest and self-confident child.

3. What are natural and logical consequences and how do they come about?

    Answer:

    - *Natural consequences* occur without any kind of intervention from you. These are events that take place as a direct result of the child's decision and they will have a profound learning impact.

    - *Logical consequences* are those that require your intervention. They would not happen on their own.

4. What considerations should be included when giving a choice?

    Answer:

    - *When* a task is to be done (Do you want to have your bath before dinner or after?)

    OR

    - *How* a task is to be done (Do you want a bath with or without bubbles?)

    OR

    - *With whom* a task is to be done (Do you want me or your dad to help with your bath?)

    BUT

    - *Not whether* the task is to be done.

    AND

    - *Choices must be age-appropriate.*

5. What are the key issues to consider in designing logical consequences?

    Answers:

    - Before applying a logical consequence, make sure a choice has been provided or implied.

    - Make sure the consequence is related to the behavior in question. The child must be able to see the connection between his or her choices and the resulting consequences.

- Once a consequence is designed, follow through with it.

- Present the consequence without anger or blame.

- Time-outs can be a logical consequence.

- Always look for a natural consequence first.

Resources

Teaching Your Children Values by Linda and Richard Eyre. 1993. New York: Simon & Schuster.

Teaching Strategies

❤ Assign chapter 7 reading (*Easy*)

Quickies and Openers

❤ Choice and Consequence Web (*Easy*)

Purpose: This opener is designed to raise students' awareness that everyday life requires the responsible management of choices and consequences.

Instructions: Write the following on the chalkboard or a huge piece of butcher paper:

Situation: Going to the game and out for pizza with friends on Friday night.	
Possible choices	Possible consequences

Ask the class to think of possible choices that might arise as this evening unfolds. Here are some activities they might suggest:

- Drive?

- Walk?

- Use an illegal substance?

- Stay sober?

- Follow laws?

- Break laws?

- Get home on time?

- Stay out later than allowed?

Write all of the possible choices on the left side of the board.

Ask students to think of the possible consequences (positive and negative) that could result from each of these choices. List these on the right side, drawing a line from the choice on the left to its possible consequence on the right.

Debrief: The material on the board presents a kind of visual representation of the "tangled webs we weave" in daily life. We make many decisions every day. There are many options from which to choose and after an option is chosen, it becomes a choice, and there are positive and negative consequences to every choice.

❤ Would You ...? (*Easy*)

Purpose: This opener illustrates the cumulative learning that can take place as a result of choosing behaviors and experiencing the consequences of those choices as we grow up.

Instructions: Have your whole class stand up. Designate one side of the classroom as the "Yes" side. Tell students that they will walk to that side of the room if they would do the behavior that you describe. Designate the other side as the "No" side. Tell students that they will walk to that side of the room if they would *not* do the behavior that you describe.

Begin by saying "Would you ..." before you read each of the following behaviors, one at a time, giving the whole class a chance to move their bodies to the "Yes" or "No" side of the room.

Would you ...

- Pull a dog's tail?

- Come to class every day if you wanted to get an "A"?

- Leave home without letting your family know where you are going?

- Wash a brand new red sweatshirt with your white clothes?

- Shower on a regular basis?

- Hide food under your bed?

- Leave your school bag or backpack on the bus?

Ask all the students to return to their seats.

There is a good chance that your whole class might move en masse to the "Yes" or "No" sides, agreeing on their willingness (or lack of) to practice each of these behaviors. You will see that these are all behaviors they have learned the consequences of from past experience, either personally or by observation.

Debrief: Ask, "Why were most of you unwilling to pull a dog's tail?" and "Why were most of you unwilling to hide food under your bed?" and/or "I noticed that most of you give yourselves showers on a regular basis. Why is that . . . ?" These questions should ignite a lively discussion and many reasons will be given. Ask students if they can draw connections between this activity and the ideas discussed in chapter 7.

Here's the connection: *We all learn from experiencing or observing consequences.* Have students reflect on the difference between the way a teenager would approach a decision vs. the way a child would approach the same decision. For example, in the decision whether to pull a dog's tail or not, a teen most likely learned a while ago that there would be the risk of being bitten. A child might do it and be bitten because children don't expect dogs to become irritated by tail pulling. *Place special emphasis on the sense of responsibility that can be gained each time we successfully or unsuccessfully encounter choices and their consequences.* The behavior of letting your family know where you are going when you leave the house is a good example of acting responsibly to reach a desired outcome and to avoid unwanted consequences.

I recommend doing the Choice and Consequence Web and Would You . . . ? openers either on the same day, or on two successive days. These exercises not only raise awareness, they also establish the basic rationale for using choices and consequences in parenting and other relationships.

Isabel's Little Lie (*Easy*)

Purpose: Stories like this raise emotions and give credence to the chapter concepts.

Instructions: Read the story, "Isabel's Little Lie," on page 49 of *Teaching Your Children Values* by Linda and Richard Eyre (see Resources earlier in this chapter).

Debrief: This story drives the point home that our choices have consequences. You might want to mention that stories like this are a good way to teach school-age children about consequences and values (in this case, honesty).

Note: It might interest your class if you tell them that in 1997 three teenagers were found guilty of involuntary manslaughter in a case where they had stolen a stop sign. Their theft resulted in a fatal auto accident where another teenager was killed.

Knowledge

❤ Essential Questions (*Easy*)

Purpose: To help students identify and organize the important points from chapter 7.

Instructions: Use **Handout 44**. The question sheet is the only teaching strategy to use for this particular chapter. It zeros in on the concepts referred to in the objectives.

The answers are given on pages 74–76 in the Chapter Overview. Perhaps you can make an overhead transparency from these pages so that students can check their own answers.

CAASE Work

❤ Collage of Choices (*Average*)

Purpose: Students show their understanding of chapter concepts by translating these ideas into a visual explanation.

Instructions: Use **Handout 45**. Give students a large piece of plain paper. You can provide materials for the collage or finding materials can be done as homework. Explain that they will do two different collages, so their paper must be divided into two halves.

❤ Free Write (*Average*)

Purpose: To stimulate personal responses about choices and consequences. The students will examine the impact of making decisions and experiencing the consequences of their choices in their own lives.

Instructions: This assignment can be done on lined paper, in existing journals, diaries, and so forth. Give students about twenty minutes to write about one of the following events. Use **Overhead 10** to list the events and explain the assignment.

- The worst decision you ever made.
- The best decision you ever made.
- A consequence that you learned the most from.
- A consequence that brought you happiness.

- A horrible consequence that caused you to feel bad about yourself.

- A consequence you experienced which taught you the value of something or someone.

- A time when you were completely confused and could not choose.

- A time when you experienced a consequence caused by a decision made by a friend.

- A time when you became a more responsible person because of a consequence you experienced.

Announce that it is important to describe (a) the event, (b) their feelings about the event, and (c) the role and influence of their parents. Then, ask them to (d) examine and describe the lasting impact that the experience had on them. They can write "confidential" on the top of the paper if they don't want you to read the details OR you can choose not to collect these. The point is to have students think deeply about personal choices they have already made and the consequences they have already experienced. If you choose not to collect their work, you might walk around the room just to check that the assignment was done.

OR

You could hold a ten-minute free write each day, giving a different topic each day.

Debrief: For this exercise, just hold a relaxed discussion of choices and consequences in our own lives. Ask students to share their experiences, but don't make it a mandatory aspect of the discussion. Be sure to draw the connections between choices and consequences and our self-esteem and sense of responsibility.

❤ Compose a Jingle (*Challenging*)

Purpose: Students must analyze the component parts of the two kinds of consequences.

Instructions: Help students form pairs to do this assignment. Explain that their task will be to write a jingle (song) to promote the practice of offering choices and consequences instead of giving punishment. Use **Handout 46**.

Debrief: Allow pairs to sing or recite their jingle for the class. You may be amazed at how willing your students will be to sing in front of the class! And . . . their jingles may be very creative.

Note: All the activities that require students to work in pairs and groups prepare them for the college and workplace experiences of the twenty-first century where skillful teamwork will be essential.

❤ Valid Choice Checklist (*Challenging*)

Purpose: Students will propose valid choices in specific situations

Instructions: Use **Handout 47**.

❤ Home Remedies (*Challenging*)

Purpose: Students rate the validity of choices and consequences presented in real-life situations.

Instructions: Use one of the following activities to expose students to real-life situations where children were offered choices and were allowed to experience consequences.

1. Invite a panel of parents and/or child-care providers to come to class to share some of the ways they apply choices and consequences.

    OR

2. Have students give examples of choices and consequences applied in their own families.

    OR

3. Have students collect examples from television shows.

    OR

4. Make a list of some of the discipline "horror stories" you've heard over the years.

   After an example is given, hold a discussion of its effectiveness in accordance with the standards presented in chapter 7. Your goal is to challenge students to rate the validity of offering choices and allowing children to experience consequences.

Another Option: A visiting preschool teacher might explain her center's procedures for offering choices and allowing children to experience consequences, including how teachers are trained to give choices. She might also cite a specific example: For example, children are asked to take turns on the teeter-totter. They are told that if they choose to hit or push, they will not be able to play on that toy for the rest of the day. Your class would ask questions and discuss the effectiveness of this practice, considering the standards presented in chapter 7. Obviously, there will be more debate over the less professional approaches to discipline—the discipline "horror stories."

Responsibility Chart (*Challenging*)

Purpose: Students verify the usefulness of choices and consequences in teaching responsibility.

Instructions: Use **Handout 48**. The completed chart will become part of the student's Portfolio.

This can be done as an in-class project or as homework.

Materials Needed: Supply poster board, Velcro, felt-tip pens. Students can procure the more exotic supplies that they might want to use.

Chapter Eight

Choosing Your Strategy

Chapter Overview

Goal

In this chapter you will learn to distinguish who owns the problem from those who don't own it, and then to determine which skills would be most effective under the particular circumstances.

Objective

At the end of this lesson you will

- Know how to use the decision tree to determine who owns the problem and the appropriate communication skill that applies to the situation

Rationale

This chapter demonstrates the interrelationship of the skills introduced in chapters 3, 4, 5, 6, and 7. You have learned how to:

- Practice active listening

- Express yourself

- Give choices and set consequences, and

- Solve problems

Using all of these skills can help you to build better relationships with everyone in your life. But sometimes it is difficult to know what to say and do when a problem situation arises. This chapter introduces the decision tree, a diagram that shows which skill to apply based on your analysis of who owns the problem. It is another skill that will help you to deal with daily relationship issues.

Essential Question and Answer

How do you decide what role to play and which skill to apply in any given situation?

Answer: You can use the decision tree to apply communication skills based on who owns the problem.

Resources

This would be a great time to take a field trip to a business where the personnel department has an established conflict-resolution process. See it live!

Teaching Strategies

Quickies and Openers

♥ A Potato Came Between You! (*Average*)

Purpose: Students are put in the position of having to use communication skills to solve a problem.

Instructions: Have students clear their desktops, putting away all materials. Divide the class into groups of eight. Pass out one potato to four students in each group of eight (four students in each group will not get a potato). Instruct students to make no marks on the potato whatsoever!

Give the Potato Meisters three to four minutes to examine their pet potatoes. Ask them to become so familiar with their potato that they would be able to recognize it later. Then, have students put their potato pets in a pile in the center of their group. Mix them up!

Now, the formerly potatoless group members get to pick up any pet potato out of the pile.

Instruct the four Potato Meisters to determine which pet potato is theirs and to negotiate for its return. Advise the potato holders to take the attitude that they want to keep the pet potato. Announce: This situation might be analogous to losing a pet in your neighborhood and realizing that a total stranger has adopted it and doesn't want to give it back. Allow four to five minutes for the negotiations.

Then, have all students return to their seats.

Debrief: Ask two, three, or four pairs to report. What happened to start their negotiation? How did the negotiation proceed? What was the result? Let it all come out. Did it get intense? Did it feel uncomfortable? Hopeless? Frustrating? OR perhaps some pairs were able to apply their relationship skills and solved the problem!

Try to find out if any students stopped to ask themselves, "Whose problem is it?" The main thing to determine is whether they applied any of the communication and problem-solving skills learned in previous chapters. Discuss the fact that if you begin by determining "Whose problem it is," that can give you direction on how to proceed, and how to know which skill is appropriate in this situation.

Knowledge

 Assign chapter 8 reading (*Easy*)

Purpose: Exercise 1 will be done as a class assignment later.

Instructions: Have students read through Emile and Angela's story and tell them to stop reading at Exercise 1.

💜 Decision Tree Business Card (*Easy*)

Purpose: Students list the facts of the decision tree.

Instructions: Use **Handout 49**. Students make copies of the business card to put in their Portfolios. They put the original business card in their wallets to refer to in real-life problem situations. You could help students acquire lamination or supply clear contact paper to make the cards more durable.

CAASE Work

❤ Exercise 1 (*Challenging*)

Purpose: Students use the decision tree to decide who owns the problem and to determine which response would be most effective.

Instructions: Post the instructions using **Overhead 11**. Help students form pairs. The members of each pair will take turns reading and deciding what to do in the situations presented in Exercise 1 in chapter 8 of the student reader of *Kids Today, Parents Tomorrow*. Ask them to get out their decision tree business card to use in this activity. Follow these steps:

1. The first person in the pair reads situation 1 aloud. Referring to their decision tree business cards, they decide who owns the problem and then describe to their partner what response they would start with to solve the problem.

   Ask students to refrain from reading the Example Answers until later.

2. Then, the second person reads situation 2 aloud. Referring to their decision tree business cards, they decide who owns the problem and then they describe to their partner what response they would start with to solve the problem.

   And so on, until they have discussed all six of the situations.

3. Students can then go on to read the Example Answers given at the end of the chapter and the chapter conclusion.

❤ Real Life (*Challenging*)

Purpose: Students apply the use of the decision tree to an actual event in their lives.

Instructions: Ask students to use the decision tree procedure in some actual event in their home lives. Ask them to write a paragraph describing how they used the decision tree approach. They should include their evaluation of the usefulness of this procedure. This could be a regular assignment or done for extra credit.

Chapter Nine

Coping with Anger

Chapter Overview

Goal

In this chapter you will learn why and how we become angry and nine ways to reduce anger.

Objectives

At the end of this lesson you will

- Understand the negative influence that anger, including physical violence, can have on a relationship

- Know why anger surfaces as a response to stressful feelings

- Understand how trigger thoughts ignite stressful feelings into anger

- Know nine ways to reduce your anger

Rationale

Many parents are concerned about the frequency and intensity, including the use of corporal punishment, with which they express anger toward their children. To children, parental anger is frightening and causes them to feel unsafe and that their parents are out of control. In relationships between adults, anger also has tremendous costs. It is one of the hardest emotions with which human beings must cope. Giving in to anger can have violent, devastating consequences. It is essential that we take responsibility for decreasing the anger and potential violence in the world, beginning with the anger within ourselves.

Essential Questions and Answers

1. Why is learning to cope with anger important to building relationships, especially the parent-child relationship?

   Answer: Parenting is a twenty-four-hour-a-day job. Anyone might occasionally feel angry as a result of this constant responsibility. But children respond to anger by becoming fearful and feeling unsafe and that their environment is out of control.
   Anger begets more anger. And it can lead to abuse. Children exposed to a lot of anger are more likely to express anger in aggressive ways than are children who are not. In adult relationships, anger can cause defensiveness and increased anger, which can lead to violence. Anger can diminish the satisfaction gained from a relationship.

2. Why do we get angry?

   Answer: When you are really stressed, getting angry can make you feel better. It works either by relieving (discharging) the tension of other painful feelings and unmet needs or desires, or by blocking awareness of those feelings. When you are anxious, you feel vulnerable and helpless, but when you are angry, you feel less vulnerable and much more powerful. By getting angry, you can block your own awareness of your anxious feelings.

3. How do we get angry? What happens that causes the transition from one feeling to a state of anger?

   Answer: There are two essential requirements to produce an angry state: stress and trigger thoughts. Neither stress nor trigger thoughts alone will lead to anger. *Trigger thoughts are those thoughts that ignite stressful feelings into anger.* They are usually thoughts that ascribe negative traits to the person with whom you are angry. They infer negative intent to his or her behavior, or they magnify the behavior to intolerable proportions. Trigger thoughts allow you to shift responsibility for your own painful feelings onto someone else, and then to justify your anger toward that person.

4. How can an individual reduce his or her anger?

Answer: Recognizing your trigger thoughts and changing them is an essential part of coping with anger. Here are nine ways to reduce your angry responses:

Changing What You Say to Yourself—Changing Your Trigger Thoughts

- Develop a coping statement that will help you keep your cool.

- *Assess the real cause of the behavior.* Recognize that all people behave in their own unique ways because everyone has a different temperament. Also, remember that everyone's behavior is an attempt to get their needs met.

- *Replace negative labels with neutral descriptions.* Avoid name calling and negative terms that feed your anger. Replace negative labels with clear, accurate descriptions of what's happening.

- *Realistically assess the magnitude of the problem.* Avoid thinking such thoughts as "This is outrageous," or "She did this just to annoy me."

Changing What You Do—Changing Your Behavior

- *Use a time-out to prevent the situation from escalating and to think about an appropriate response.* Take a time-out yourself to calm down, and give children time-outs to allow them to calm down, *or* to serve as a consequence for misbehavior.

- *Practice relaxation through deep breathing.* Because deep breathing requires expansion of the chest and belly, and facilitates the slow, full replenishing of oxygen to the lungs, it is the antidote to stress and, therefore, a valuable tool in the struggle against anger.

- *Identify what you need and ask for it in an assertive way.* Once you can identify the feeling behind your anger, ask yourself what you need to do to take care of that feeling. Once you've identified what you need, ask for it assertively.

- *Plan ahead.* Anticipate a situation that might trigger your anger. Plan a coping strategy. This reduces the chances of being caught off guard by the unexpected.

- *Get support.* This means knowing how to take care of yourself. See chapter 10.

5. What is the definition of physical abuse?

Answer: Physical abuse is corporal punishment that results in bruises, welts, or other injuries.

6. Describe some ways that parents psychologically abuse their children.

> Answer: A parent who constantly yells at a child, belittles the child, calls the child names, threatens to hurt or abandon the child, or hurts or damages someone or something in front of the child is psychologically abusing that child.

Teaching Strategies

Assign chapter 9 reading (*Easy*)

Quickies and Openers

 Art Imitating Life (*Easy*)

Purpose: To raise awareness of the various forms that anger can take.

Instructions: Play a clip from a movie or video that shows a scene where the characters are acting out feelings of displeasure, anger, or rage. OR have students read a passage from a novel where feelings of displeasure, anger, or rage are described.

 Life Imitating Art (*Easy*)

Purpose: To remind students of the anger they have felt and what triggered those feelings of anger.

Instructions: Ask students to write for fifteen minutes describing a time in their lives when they experienced a feeling of anger similar to what they saw in the movie or video clip, or to what they read about in the novel.

Knowledge

❤ Just the Facts, Ma'am (*Easy*)

Purpose: Use this activity to recall some of the facts that define anger.

Instructions: Use **Handout 50**. These are the same essential questions that were presented in the chapter overview. High school students will be highly challenged to get complete answers. Therefore, it will be important to go over the answers as a class. Notice that essential questions 5 and 6 are not included on this handout. You may want to define physical and psychological abuse and note that they may result from anger.

CAASE Work

Current Events (*Average*)

Purpose: Students will demonstrate their understanding of some of the psychological dynamics of anger.

Instructions: Ask your students to read the newspaper and find one story that reports on violent behavior that resulted from someone's angry feelings. Ask students to cut out the story and bring it to class. Read several out loud. After reading a few, ask students whether there were any clues in the stories as to the violent person's stressors or possible trigger thoughts.

The "A" Collection (*Easy*)

Purpose: The students will record events surrounding their own feelings of anger

Instructions: Use **Handout 51**. For one week, ask your students to identify and record each event that makes them feel angry. You will need to give very thorough instructions to get them started.

Aztec Codex (*Easy*)

Purpose: Students will make an Aztec codex, or fold-out picture book, which lists the two requirements for anger (stress and trigger thoughts) and the nine ways to reduce anger.

Materials Needed:

> White butcher paper, cut into 50" x 3" strips, one per student
>
> OR
>
> Ten 3" x 5" index cards, taped together end to end, for each student
>
> White poster board, cut into 6" x 4" pieces, two per student
>
> Glue
>
> Markers, crayons, or paint to apply Aztec designs on front and back covers

Instructions: Use **Handout 52**. This will go into the students' Portfolios. Provide some background.

The Aztecs lived in Mexico from about 1300 A.D. to 1500 A.D. A codex is a fold-out picture book written by an Aztec scribe or writer. Typically, a codex contained pictures and symbols and was used to record calendars, histories, creation stories, or events from the daily life of the Aztec people.

❤ Educational Film (*Challenging*)

Purpose: The students will show their mastery of the content of chapter 9 by creating an informational video.

Instructions: Use **Handout 53**. Divide the class into five equal groups. Randomly assign the following topics to the groups:

- Why learning to cope with anger is important to building relationships, especially the parent-child relationship.

- Why people get angry.

- How people get angry. What happens that causes the transition from one feeling to a state of anger?

- How can an individual reduce his/her angry feelings?

- Four ways to change what you say to yourself; changing your trigger thoughts.

- Five ways to change what you do; changing your behavior.

Later provide the video cameras as needed. Allow plenty of time for the completion of the project. Show the videos in the numerical order of the topics to achieve a logical presentation of the information.

Optional: Edit the pieces of video produced by each group into one continuous tape. Ask each student to bring a blank videotape and make copies for each student's Portfolio.

❤ Free Write (*Average*)

Purpose: Students discuss the effectiveness of the suggestions for coping with anger.

Instructions: Ask the students to recall a very recent event that may have aroused feelings of anger in them. Then ask if any students, after reading chapter 9, had been able to recognize their trigger thoughts. Follow this question by asking whether any students had been able to change their trigger thoughts by any of the nine ways to reduce anger. Ask the students to write about the event and describe how they applied the suggestions for coping with anger. How effective were the techniques? Would they use them again in the future?

Materials Needed: Pass out lined paper.

Chapter Ten

Taking Care of
Yourself

Chapter Overview

Goal

This chapter will help you develop ways of nurturing yourself whether or not you are now—or eventually become—a parent.

Objective

At the end of this lesson you will

- Know, and hopefully be practicing, many ways to nurture yourself

Rationale

Nurturing yourself is an essential life skill, whether you are a parent or not. Being a student, holding a job, and helping maintain a household all require hard work, and it is easy to forget that it is your responsibility to keep a healthy balance between work and play in your life. Parenting may be the hardest job of all, but it also can be one of the most rewarding. Taking care of yourself enables you to maintain your strength not only to cope with the endless hours and worries, but also to reap the rewards. The more you incorporate self-nurturing habits and routines into your daily life, the more energy and joy you will have to give to your children and other relationships.

Essential Questions and Answers

1. Why is it important to take care of yourself?

   Answer: You need nurturing just as much as children need it partly because the older you are, the more your life becomes complex and occasionally burdensome. However, the responsibility for nurturing now rests on your own shoulders. Nurturing yourself is essential to your well-being.

2. What are some ways to nurture yourself?

   - Take time for yourself just to rest, read, take bubble baths, listen to music, or do whatever feels nurturing.

   - Regularly make time to talk and share your thoughts, feelings, frustrations, and so forth with a partner or friend.

   - Do something fun/stimulating/challenging with a friend, partner, or by yourself.

   - Treat yourself to a little pampering occasionally.

   - Eat well.

   - Get enough exercise.

   - Get enough sleep.

   - Let some things go. If you have a partner in parenting, it will probably be a lot easier to accomplish some of these suggestions than if you are a single parent.

   - If you are a single parent, getting support from your family, friends, or community is essential for your well-being and your child's.

Resources

Check the resources available in your community. You may find organizations such as Parental Stress, Parents Without Partners, and Parents Anonymous that provide services to stressed parents.

Teaching Strategies

 Assign chapter 10 reading (*Easy*)

Quickies and Openers

 Reflection (*Easy*)

Purpose: To review the many ways of nurturing.

Instructions: Ask students to remember back to their childhood to recall ways they were nurtured as children. You could ask them to do a free write, share with one other class member, or share with the entire class. **Note:** Before doing this activity, you might want students to review the ways to nurture in chapter 1.

Debrief: Postdiscussion activities should include a reminder that we learn to nurture ourselves by the way we were (or were not) nurtured in our childhood. If we didn't learn nurturing ways or we have forgotten them, we need to renew the practice of self-nurturing in our lives.

 Relaxation Exercise (*Easy*)

Purpose: Students experience the positive effects of a stress-relieving activity.

Instructions: Acquire a relaxation tape for the class to follow as an exercise. I recommend *Body Scan* by Mark Neenan, M. Ed. He leads mindfulness-based stress reduction groups at hospitals in the San Francisco Bay Area. On side one of the *Body Scan* tape, Mr. Neenan leads the listener through a progressive relaxation of the body and, on the other side, he leads the listener through a "sitting meditation." Each side of the tape is forty-five minutes long.

To purchase a copy of the *Body Scan* tape, write to: Mark Neenan, M. Ed., The Wood House, 2161 Empire Grade, Santa Cruz, CA 95060.

Enclose $10.00, which includes shipping and handling.

OR

You can purchase various types of relaxation tapes at many bookstores, health stores, and yoga centers.

Advance Preparation: Listen to the tape in advance at home where you can become familiar with the peaceful sensations of this type of relaxation. It is important to *stay awake and center your thoughts on breathing and relaxing parts of your body during the tape. If other thoughts come to mind, allow them to pass. Do not dwell on any thoughts and try to focus on your breathing.*

Make arrangements to meet your class in a dance studio, wrestling room, or other gymnastics room because you will need enough space and mats for everyone to lie on their backs comfortably. OR you can play the tape while students sit in their chairs, eyes closed, in a somewhat darkened classroom.

With Students: Pass out pieces of paper and ask students to write five words that describe the current state of their mind and/or body (for example, tense, tired, stressed, loose, etc.).

Tell your students that they will be listening to a tape designed to specifically help them relax their bodies and minds. Read aloud the italicized instructions in the paragraph labeled "Advance Preparation" above, and remind students to be respectful of others' efforts by not speaking. If someone is opposed to participating, he or she may lie down or sit quietly nearby. Mark Neenan's tape is forty-five-minutes long, but you do not need to complete the tape to experience some of the benefits of relaxation. Any other tape will be as long, so begin as soon as possible or arrange to have a longer class session that day.

Debrief: After the exercise, allow students some quiet time to open their eyes and return to a sitting position. Ask them to turn their pieces of paper to the blank side and to write down five words that describe their minds and/or bodies after the relaxation exercise. Discuss their impressions of the activity. How do their bodies feel after the relaxation? Do they notice any changes in their state of mind or body? *The goal of this opener is to raise awareness of what it means to take time for yourself, and to impress on students the idea that taking time for yourself does have beneficial results for you and your relationships.*

Free Write (*Easy*)

Purpose: Students examine the nurturing effects of activities they enjoy doing.

Instructions: Ask students to think about an activity they enjoy doing, such as reading, being alone, or listening to music. Allow them to write about it for ten minutes. Write the following on the board:

- What do you enjoy doing?

- How often do you get a chance to do this activity?

- Is this activity something you do on a regular basis?

- Why do you enjoy it? How does it make you feel?

- Do you think this activity will continue to be part of your life? Why? Why not?

Knowledge

🖤 Essential Elephant (*Easy*)

Purpose: Students extract and list the main points from chapter 10.

Instructions: Use **Handout 54**. This is just another way to get students to focus on the main points in the chapter, which in this case, are suggestions of ways to nurture yourself. This elephant list could be added to the Portfolio.

🖤 Community Service Video (*Challenging*)

Purpose: Students make a video for couples going through prepared childbirth classes at local hospitals. The objectives of the video are: (a) to communicate the idea that parents need to nurture themselves to enhance their performance as parents and, (b) to give suggestions for self-nurturing.

Instructions: Use **Handout 55**. Divide the class into teams and give each team one of the concepts from chapter 10: the reasons that everyone, especially parents, should nurture themselves AND each of the ten ways to self-nurture that are described in the chapter. (You may even think of more.)
Ask each team to develop a short vignette to demonstrate their concept. The vignettes could be done in any style; for example, teams could interview a parent or couple who practice that form of taking care of themselves. Students could use narration over pictures, or they could act out the concept.

Production Notes: Integrate this exercise with the Theater Arts department of your school to jointly produce the video(s). Check with your county's Office of Education, they may have a video specialist or a video crew in their media department that might be able to help.

OR

🖤 A Different Community Service Video (*Challenging*)

Purpose: Students make the same type of video described above; however, they make it for high school or college students instead of for expectant parents.

Instructions: Use **Handout 56** and change the language where necessary.

OR

 Display (*Average*)

Purpose: Students make a display for school, a medical office or clinic, a teen health center, or a public library to communicate the need for self-nurturing.

Instructions: Use **Handout 56**.

OR

Feature Article (*Challenging*)

Purpose: Students write articles for a newspaper or newsletter.

Instructions: Use **Handout 57**.

CAASE Work

Application Activities

1. **Teach a Lesson on Nutrition:** If you are not a Science or a Home Economics Careers and Technology teacher, you may want to ask someone from those departments to help you plan a brief lesson on nutrition. You could also invite a volunteer from the American Dietetics Association or a registered nurse to present the basics of personal nutrition. The Dairy Council and Heart Association have good materials.

   I have met many young adults who have told me that the one piece lacking in their formal education was the everyday application of the science of nutrition. I have also heard from many former students that they will be eternally grateful for the information about nutrition that they learned in our nutrition and foods classes. (Thanks to my teaching partner, Margie!) The study of nutrition was removed or reduced in high schools whenever Home Economics courses were reduced. Making healthy food choices and preparing food for a family is one of the greatest responsibilities of parenthood, as well as being a personal health responsibility.

2. **Daily Stretching:** Work with your Physical Education Department to show your students how to do a daily stretching routine that can be practiced in the morning and/or at night to relax and feel better or to prepare muscles for physical exercise.

3. **Sleep:** Get help from your Health teacher to present a lesson on sleep. There is much new research on the importance of sleep and the human minimum requirements for sleep.

4. **Panel:** Invite a panel of single parents to talk about their daily lives. You could also do a mixed panel of single parents and parenting couples. Ask them to comment on their ability to take care of themselves and the responsibilities of parenthood.

5. **Keep a Journal:** Have students keep a journal for a week, making a concerted effort to practice some sort of self-nurturing activity each day, and writing about it in their journals. Encourage them to write about all aspects of trying to add a new dimension to their daily routine: remembering to do it, time, interruptions, how it makes them feel, problems, rewards, and so forth.

Chapter Eleven

Special Problems of
the Young Parent

Chapter Overview

Goal

This chapter explores some of the many issues young parents must face.

Objective

At the end of this lesson you will be more aware of some of the issues faced by young parents.

Rationale

As hard as it is to be a parent, it is even harder to be a very young parent. Not only do young parents face the challenges of raising a child, they also face the task of completing their own development and growth into adulthood. This chapter explores some of the issues faced by such young parents, and, as such, it may be helpful to someone who is thinking about becoming a young parent.

Essential Question and Answers

What are some of the special problems facing the young parent?
Answers:

- Making the decision to keep the baby

- Feeling prepared for parenthood

- Coping with the physical and emotional responsibilities

- Surviving the sacrifices

- Asking for help and support

- Kids raising kids

Teaching Strategies

This is a simple and straightforward chapter. There is no skill to be developed on the part of the learner. Concepts are meant to be presented only for awareness. There is, therefore, no need to take a skill-development stance with this material. However, you do want to engage students with the ideas presented. Here are a few possibilities:

❤ Assign chapter 11 reading (*Easy*)

1. Invite a panel of speakers to do a presentation:

   - A representative from an adoption agency. TOPIC: Adoption Agencies/Various Forms of Adoption

   - An adoptive parent. TOPIC: The Experiences of an Adoptive Parent

   - A birth parent. TOPIC: The Experiences of a Birth Parent

2. Invite a panel of young parents, fathers and mothers, to share their experiences.

3. Try this variation on the panel of young parents: Form a panel of people who became parents in their teen years, but who are now in their twenties, thirties, forties, or fifties. They would have a variety of perspectives on the social ramifications of their choice to become parents in earlier decades, the motives behind their decisions, their impressions of readiness for parenting, and the overall impact that the experience of young parenthood had on their lives.

4. Invite a panel of speakers from agencies that provide support to young parents. Call your county Health Department, county hospital, and/or Department of Public Social Services to see what's available in your community.

To prepare for a guest speaker visit:

Always announce at least one day in advance that speakers are coming and ask students to write one question they might have for the speaker. Collect questions and have them ready to ask in case they are not answered during the speaker's presentation.

As a thank-you gift, give each guest speaker a copy of the "Taking Care of Yourself" video that your class produced for chapter 10.

❤ Application for a Parenting License (*Challenging*)

Purpose: Students assess the skills needed to be an effective parent and create a scale with which prospective parents can evaluate their readiness for parenthood.

Instructions: Use **Handout 58**. To prepare the students to create an application, you might want to visit various agencies to get samples of different types of applications for the students to use as models.

Le Finale!

Award a "Prepared for Parenting" certificate to students who complete the *Kids Today, Parents Tomorrow* curriculum and/or have completed a Portfolio.

Chapter 1

HANDOUT 1

Silver Jewel Box Pattern for Beads of Oman

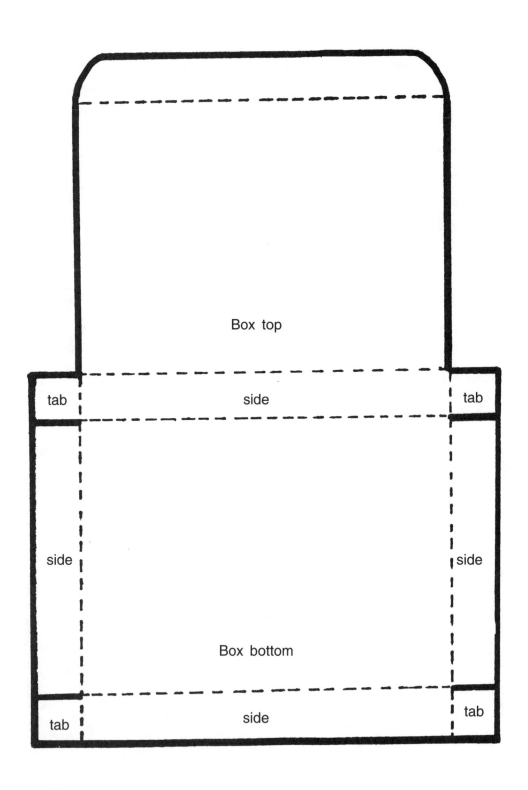

Box top

tab   side   tab

side   Box bottom   side

tab   side   tab

Place a piece of carbon paper between the pattern on the opposite page, and the cardboard; pin or tape the pattern and carbon paper to the cardboard.

Press firmly to trace the solid cutting lines and the dotted folding lines.

Remove the pattern and the carbon paper.

Cut on the outer solid line; clip the four inner solid lines.

Fold on the dotted lines. Fold corner tabs to the inside and glue or staple in place.

Smooth foil over the box, using glue where necessary. Don't worry about folds and wrinkles, they create the appearance of tarnished silver.

Optional: Wipe on a bit of black tempera. Wipe off excess paint.

HANDOUT 2

Notetaking

Taking notes during reading and class lectures can make you a better student. Here's how good notes can help you:

- Taking notes helps you remember the material. Learning the material is more important than the grade you earn.

- Taking notes will make class more interesting because you are involved.

- Notes can be used to review for a test or to complete a learning activity.

- Using notes will help you get higher grades.

Nine Guidelines for Notetaking

1. Use lined notebook paper.

2. Leave a 2-inch margin on the left side of the paper to <u>summarize the main points</u> of the lecture or reading, to <u>make personal comments</u>, or to <u>fill in missing information</u>.

3. Put the following information on the first page of each set of notes:

    - Your Name

    - Title or Topic of Lecture or Reading

    - Course/Period

    - Date

    - Number of Pages in this Set of Notes

4. Be brief. Do not write every word. Summarize and paraphrase. Summarizing and paraphrasing increases your understanding of the material and makes your review easier. Note: Some items, like definitions, quotes, and technical terms, must be written out completely.

5. Use abbreviations and symbols. Add ones that you already use to this list and put it in the front of your notebook:

r = are	u = you	@ = at
w/ = with	w/o = without	# = number
↑ = increase	↓ = decrease	/ = per
> = more than	< = less than	
+ = and	= is	

6. If you miss something during a lecture, leave a space and put a "?" in the margin to remind yourself to ask for that information after class.

7. If you think of a question during a lecture, write it in the margin and ask it after the lecture.

8. The teacher usually writes important points on the chalkboard—copy this information into your notes!

9. Write legibly with a pen.

EXAMPLE

How to Set Up a Piece of Notebook Paper for Notetaking

_____

Name _____ Topic _____

Course _____ Period _____ Date _____ # Pages _____

Main points, Comments, Questions	**NOTES**

HANDOUT 3

Essential Questions

PERIOD _____ NAME _____

1. What is nurturing?

2. What is physical nurturing?

3. What is emotional nurturing?

4. How do we provide emotional nurturing to others? List the six essential components of emotional nurturing and write a brief description of each.

5. What benefits does a child receive from emotional nurturing?

Chapter 1

HANDOUT 4

Whodunit?

PERIOD _____ NAME _____

For each of the following components of nurturing, identify a person, other than a parent, who performs this type of nurturing as a part of his or her role in society. List six different people by the name of their role or job, not by personal name (Example: Teacher). In the right column, give a specific example of how each person practices this form of nurturing.

	A person who nurtures as part of his or her role or job	An example of something they do to practice nurturing
Attention		
Mirroring		
Understanding		
Acceptance and respect for who they are		
Soothing their pain		
Fostering self-esteem		

HANDOUT 5

Haiku

PERIOD _____ NAME _____

Use this activity to examine the role that nurturing has played in your life. Write at least two specific examples of the ways your parents and others nurture you.

ATTENTION

1.

2.

MIRRORING

1.

2.

UNDERSTANDING

1.

2.

ACCEPTANCE AND RESPECT FOR WHO YOU ARE

1.

2.

SOOTHING YOUR PAIN

1.

2.

FOSTERING SELF-ESTEEM

1.

2.

From what you listed above, pick about ten words or phrases that best represent the ways you have been nurtured.

1.

2.

3.

4.

5.

6.

7.

8.

9.

10.

Write a HAIKU poem using words and phrases selected from your list of ten words and/or phrases.

Here is a dictionary definition of haiku:

Hai-ku (hi-koo) noun. A poem in imitation of a Japanese verse form, consisting of three lines of five, seven, and five syllables, respectively.

Haiku poems take many forms other than the way they are described in this definition. However, using this form may make it easier for you to write a haiku poem. If you choose to use this form, your poem will have three lines: the first line will have five syllables, the second line will have seven syllables, and the third line will contain five syllables.

Here are a few suggestions for writing haiku in English:

- Nature is the domain of haiku. Nurturing is fundamental in nature; therefore, your experiences related to nurturing provide a sound basis for your haiku poem.

- Always be aware of this present moment. Haiku is about showing, not telling a story; it's about expressing what you feel in the present moment. Use words to make pictures, not statements. Do not use complete sentences. Use verbs in the present tense.

- Be true to life. Write about your experiences just as they are. Lifelikeness, not beauty, is characteristic of haiku.

- Carefully choose words that clearly express what you feel. Do not use the words "I," "me," or "myself." Do use words that suggest the time of day, place, season, or location.

- Rhyme is not characteristic of haiku. Verses should sound natural when read aloud.

- Haiku must be simple to understand. It must not be abstract or intellectual.

- Rewrite your poem until it suggests exactly what you want others to see and feel when they read it.

EXAMPLE

Young reaching for life

held safely in warm embrace

drift away in time.

HANDOUT 6

Nature/Nurture Display

PERIOD _____ NAME _____

PREPARATION

For each of the six essential components of nurturing, pick one or two key words or phrases that best describe HOW we perform that type of nurturing. Write them below.

ATTENTION

MIRRORING

Example: We show others, through our words or actions, that they are wonderful and a pleasure to be around.

UNDERSTANDING

ACCEPTANCE AND RESPECT FOR WHO THEY ARE

SOOTHING THEIR PAIN

FOSTERING SELF-ESTEEM

Take this list with you on a walk in any outdoor setting such as a park, the beach, or the woods. <u>As you walk, think about how we nurture each other.</u> Collect six IDEAS OR IMAGES from nature that have something in common with each component of nurturing. (Do not collect real objects—you can take photos or make sketches.)

List the six ideas or images that you collect and write a brief reason for selecting them. In other words, what quality or feature does the idea or image have in common with the type of nurturing?

Example: *Mirroring—A pool of water. I selected it because water reflects an image. When mirroring, we are reflecting back the pleasure that a person gives to us.*

Attention—Idea /Image _____

Reason for selecting _____

Mirroring—Idea/Image _____

Reason for selecting _____

Understanding—Idea/Image _____

Reason for selecting _____

Acceptance and respect for who they are—Idea /Image _____

Reason for selecting _____

Soothing their pain—Idea/Image _____

Reason for selecting _____

Fostering self-esteem—Idea/Image _____

Reason for selecting _____

THE DISPLAY

Make a six-part, accordion-folded "how-to" display out of cardboard or any stiff paper. The completed display should be free-standing. On <u>each </u>of the six sections of the display, include the following:

- The name of one of the essential components of emotional nurturing.

- Give your display the look of nature. Incorporate the idea or image from nature as a drawing, a photograph, a decoration, or a logo.

- In paragraph form, write your suggestions for <u>how</u> we can practice this kind of nurturing with others (especially children). To add interest to your writing and to enhance the reader's understanding, begin your paragraph with a simile between the idea from nature and the component of nurturing. (Definition: sim-i-le/noun/a figure of speech using <u>some point of resemblance</u> observed to exist between two things that differ in other respects.)

EXAMPLE:

Seeing parents who express delight in their child is like seeing your image being reflected in a pond. You look into the water, you see your image reflected by the water, and you know what you look like. When parents mirror a child, the child knows that she or he is a pleasure to be around. Mirroring is communicated by means of facial expression, gesture, and tone of voice. It can also be verbalized.

Create a display that is esthetically pleasing and draws attention. Use your artistic abilities and creativity. Give thought and planning to design elements such as color, proportion, use of space, and balance. This display can be used to educate others at school or in the community.

On the back of your display:

- Glue the first two pages of this Handout to the back of your display.

- Write a paragraph describing the name and location of your walk and why you chose the particular place that you did choose. Glue this to the back of your display.

CONTENT

Refer to the assessment rubric (Handout 7) for the performance standard expected for completion of this project.

HANDOUT 7

Assessment Rubric for Nature/Nurture Display

I. PREPARATION PRIOR TO CREATING YOUR DISPLAY   YES/NO

Completed fill-in portions of Handout 6 .... —— ——

Wrote paragraph describing name and location of walk and your reason for choosing the place .... —— ——

Collected six ideas or images from nature .... —— ——

II. THE DISPLAY

Is free-standing .... —— ——

Has one panel for each of the six essential components of emotional nurturing .... —— ——

Each panel is headed with the name of a component of nurturing .... —— ——

Each panel has a paragraph that begins with a simile and contains suggestions for <u>how</u> to practice the kind of nurturing .... —— ——

The idea or image from nature is also visually depicted on the panel .... —— ——

Has lettering that is legible and large enough to be read three feet away .... —— ——

Has first two pages of Handout 6 attached to the back .... —— ——

Attached to the back is a paragraph description of the walk location .... —— ——

SCORES:

PREPARATION PRIOR TO CREATING YOUR DISPLAY   _____

THE DISPLAY   _____

CONTENT   _____

         GRAND TOTAL   _____

         GRADE   _____

Note: The teacher will assign point values and/or letter grades to each aspect of the assessment rubric.

III. CONTENT

Performance Task	Exceptional Performer	Strong Performer	Capable Performer	Limited Performer	Nonperformer
Quality Producer: The Student Produces a Product That Reflects Craftsmanship through Artistry and Creativity	Applies personal artistry to the visuals and writing. Creates visuals that enhance the written portions. Applies design principles effectively. Produces an exciting display that attracts an audience, that is esthetically pleasing, and has the look of nature. *(cont.)*	Applies personal artistry to the visuals and writing. Creates visuals that enhance the written portions. Partially applies design principles. Produces a display that is esthetically pleasing and has the look of nature. *(cont.)*	Understands the writing and visual tasks. Creates visuals that work with the writing. Designs are adequate. Display makes sense.	Student's writing carries a message. Does not provide visuals that enhance the written portions. Does not apply design principles. Does not carry out the nature theme.	The student does not produce a Nature/Nurture Display
Literacy: The Student Demonstrates Knowledge of Nurturing as a Parenting and Relationship Skill	Shows understanding of nurturing by drawing an appropriate comparison in each simile. Writes six paragraphs outlining <u>how</u> to perform each component of nurturing. Completes the top portion of Handout 6 with key words and *(cont.)*	Shows understanding of nurturing by drawing an appropriate comparison in most of the similes. Writes six paragraphs outlining <u>how</u> to perform each component of nurturing. Completes the top portion of Handout 6 *(cont.)*	Shows some understanding of nurturing by drawing some comparisons in some paragraphs. Writes five or fewer paragraphs but does not outline how to perform each task of nurturing. *(cont.)*	Does not include a simile in each of the six paragraphs. Writes fewer than six paragraphs, but some or all do not fully outline <u>how</u> to perform each component of nurturing. Partially completes the top portion of Handout 6. *(cont.)*	The student does not produce a Nature/Nurture Display

116

III. CONTENT

Performance Task	Exceptional Performer	Strong Performer	Capable Performer	Limited Performer	Nonperformer
	phrases that describe <u>how</u> to perform each type of nurturing. Completes the bottom portion of Handout 6 with ideas and images from nature and a reason for their selection.	with key words and phrases that describe <u>how</u> to perform each type of nurturing. Completes the bottom portion of Handout 6 with ideas and images from nature and a reason for their selection.	Completes more than half of the top of Handout 6. Completes more than half of the bottom of Handout 6.	Partially completes the bottom portion of Handout 6.	
Communication: The Student Performs Communication Skills Necessary for Parenting and Other Relationships, Including Those at School, at Home, and at Work	Begins each paragraph with a simile that adds interest and enhances the reader's understanding of how to nurture. Selects ideas and images from nature that are appropriate for the purpose and audience. Writes clear and concise paragraphs. Writes without grammatical errors.	Begins each paragraph with a simile, however, the simile is not very effective in enhancing the reader's understanding of how to nurture. Selects ideas and images from nature that are appropriate for the purpose and audience. Writes clear and concise paragraphs. Writes without grammatical errors.	Begins each paragraph with a weak simile about nurturing that is not very effective, but is a simile. Selects ideas and images from nature that are appropriate for the purpose and audience. Writes paragraphs that are clear but are either too wordy or too short. Writes with some grammatical errors.	Writes paragraphs that do not communicate how to nurture. Selects ideas and images from nature that cannot be interpreted by the audience. Writes with grammatical errors.	The student does not produce a Nature/Nurture Display

HANDOUT 8

Role Play

PERIOD _____ NAME _____

Write a role play for each of the situations described below. Your play should have two characters: a parent and a child. Write about three or four lines of dialogue for each character to show how nurturing is played out in everyday life.

SITUATION 1: Franny's mom is wrapping several gifts for donation to a Toys for Tots fund-raiser. Someone will be by to pick the gifts up in less than an hour. She's giggling and playful and her mom uses the opportunity to **mirror** what an amusing, delightful child she is.

SITUATION 2: Ms. Williams is driving to the store with her son, Tyrone, sitting next to her in the car. As they drive, Tyrone describes an experience he had during recess when some older kids said he couldn't play kickball with them because he was too little. He said he felt bad about it and didn't want to go to school the next day. Ms. Williams gives Tyrone her full **attention** while he talks about his feelings.

SITUATION 3: Ms. Santos is having one of those exhausted evenings zoned out in front of the TV, thinking to herself that there can't possibly be two more whole days left in what feels like the longest week of her life. She's also thinking about how great it will be when she gets her Occupational Therapy certification and she'll be able to spend her days with people instead of machines. Her son, David, a high school senior, comes in and tells her that a neighbor has just offered him a full-time job in sales at his used car lot. David explains that he is tired of school and wants to take the job so he can buy a car and be more independent. For the past eighteen years David has been encouraged by his family to pursue higher education so that he will be able to find a more satisfying job. Ms. Santos shows her **understanding** for David's yearnings. She also clearly restates her position on the necessity for higher education.

SITUATION 4: Three-year-old Twyla won't go to sleep in her bedroom because she says there's a monster in her closet. Her dad suddenly realizes that reading *There's a Monster in My Closet* on the first day of mom's business trip was a bad idea. Twyla is sensitive and theatrical; she often plays out her feelings through "make-believe." Show how her dad **accepts and respects** her unique personality as he solves the problem and helps her settle into sleep in her own bed.

SITUATION 5: Here's an easy one! Well, maybe not! You're driving your twelve-year old to school. As you turn into the drop zone she squeals, "Eeeeeeeek!!! I forgot to collect a dozen fascinating objects for the 'Wild Thing Composition' that we're writing today!" Go ahead, **soothe her pain**!

SITUATION 6: This one *is* easy! The Chapras' fourteen-year-old daughter, Yani, has been sneaking out of the house late at night to be with friends at a local burger joint. The family rules clearly forbid being out alone after 9:00 P.M. (Not to mention that they're vegetarians!) Yani has an outgoing and playful personality. Her friends always insist that she come along, saying, "It won't be any fun without you!" She just wants to have fun and be like everybody else. She truly doesn't understand her family's rules; she thinks they don't make sense for life in this decade! Write a dialogue where the parents uphold their standards of discipline and **foster** Yani's **self-esteem** at the same time.

HANDOUT 9

Editorial

PERIOD _____ NAME _____

You are a member of the editorial board of your school newspaper. The board has just decided to publish an editorial to persuade readers to recognize the value of nurturing and to practice nurturing in their relationships, especially with children. Because you favor this viewpoint, you volunteer to write the editorial.

Writing an editorial provides you with a chance to influence community opinion. The editorial page is the one place in a newspaper where the editors try to tell readers what to think. An editorial can be very powerful and an editorial writer has responsibilities.

- Write with courage if you are positive your cause is just.

- Use a powerful and persuasive writing style. Avoid personal attacks and name-calling. Don't be arrogant or overly emotional.

- Use precise logic.

- Present facts honestly and completely.

- Your reason for writing to persuade others must be above reproach. An editorial writer must be devoted to the public welfare and to public service.

- You must state the truth as you see it and not be blinded by bias or prejudice.

The purposes of an editorial are to:

- Explain or add additional information.

- Influence the way readers think.

- Propose a possible solution in solving a problem.

- Amuse. Editorials can be essays or cartoons.

- To urge readers to adopt a specific course of action.

To write your editorial (persuasive essay):

- Prewrite: *Gather facts* about nurturing and neglect. Collect ideas from your chapter 1 activities and reading. You may also want to talk to friends and family about nurturing and neglect.

- After reviewing the facts, decide your *point of view*. Here, your point of view refers to your opinion on the practice of nurturing. Your editorial board took the position that nurturing is beneficial for relationships (especially parenting) and should be practiced.

- Write a *thesis statement*. Your thesis statement presents the subject of your argument (nurturing) and your point of view on the subject. A thesis statement appeals to the readers to do or to believe something. Your thesis statement needs to give an opinion that can be supported with sound reasoning and evidence.

- Know your *audience*. The better you know your audience, the better you will be able to make arguments which convince that audience. In this case, your audience is your peers.

- Follow the pattern of organization that you would use for any type of essay. The *introductory paragraph* introduces the main idea and usually contains your thesis statement. The *body* explains the main idea and presents reasons and evidence in support of your opinion. The body may be several paragraphs long. The *conclusion* summarizes the main points or restates the thesis in a new way.

- You may use one of the following formats to structure your essay:

Begin by stating a conclusion and then assemble the supporting facts on which your conclusion is based. Your conclusion could begin with the idea that neglect has devastating effects on children, whereas nurturing fosters healthy growth and development.

Use a current event as an opener and then move through the facts to arrive at a conclusion. You may choose a current event on the topic of child neglect.

- An editorial should be from *200 to 300 words long*.

- You will need to give your editorial a catchy and appropriate *headline*.

The copy that you turn in should be mounted on the same kind of paper as your Nature/Nurture Display. After it is evaluated and returned, it will become part of that display.

HANDOUT 10

Assessment Rubric for Editorial

PERIOD _____ NAME _____

Performance Task	Exceptional Performer	Strong Performer	Capable Performer	Limited Performer	Nonperformer
Leadership: The Student Performs the Responsibilities of an Editorial Writer	Student becomes a leader of community opinion because personal belief in the value of nurturing is courageously and powerfully stated. Writes persuasively without being arrogant or overly emotional. Avoids personal attacks. Uses precise logic. Presents facts honestly and completely. Is motivated by pursuit of public welfare and public service. Serves the truth and is free of bias. *(cont.)*	States a personal belief in the value of nurturing. Writes persuasively without being arrogant or overly emotional. Avoids personal attacks. Uses consistent logic. Presents facts honestly and completely. Is motivated by pursuit of public welfare and public service. Serves the truth and is free of bias. *(cont.)*	States a vague belief in the value of nurturing. Writes persuasively; however, tends to be arrogance or overly emotional statements. Avoids personal attacks. Uses inconsistent logic. Presents facts honestly; however, omits some facts. Is motivated by pursuit of public welfare and public service. Serves the truth and is free of bias. *(cont.)*	Does not state a personal belief in the value of nurturing. Student's persuasive writing is flawed by arrogance or overly emotional appeals. Includes personal attacks. Presents facts in an illogical manner. Omits key facts. Does not write with devotion to public welfare and public service. Does not fully serve the truth and is biased.	Student begins but fails to complete an editorial. Unable to begin effectively. Makes no attempt to begin an editorial.
Communication: Student Uses the Persuasive Writing	Writes independently and with enthusiasm. Amuses. Influences readers. Explains or adds information. *(cont.)*	Writes independently. Influences readers. Explains or adds information. Proposes a possible *(cont.)*	Writes with some guidance. Influences readers. Explains or adds information. Urges readers to *(cont.)*	Writes with a great deal of assistance. Does not influence readers. Does not explain or add information. Does not *(cont.)*	Student begins but fails to complete an editorial. *(cont.)*

Performance Task	Exceptional Performer	Strong Performer	Capable Performer	Limited Performer	Nonperformer
Process to Create an Effective Editorial	Proposes a possible solution to a problem. Urges readers to adopt a specific course of action. Student includes facts, expresses his/her point of view, composes and supports a thesis statement, and uses standard essay format (introduction, body, and conclusion). Writes between 200 and 300 words. Gives the editorial an eye-catching headline.	solution to a problem. Urges readers to adopt a specific course of action. Student includes facts, expresses his/her point of view, composes and supports a thesis statement, and uses standard essay format (introduction, body, and conclusion). Writes between 200 and 300 words. Gives the editorial a catchy headline.	adopt a specific course of action. Includes most of the facts. Expresses his/her point of view. Composes a weak thesis statement that is not supported Uses standard essay format (introduction, body, and conclusion). Writes less than 200 words or more than 300 words. Includes a headline that does not enhance the editorial.	urge readers to adopt a specific course of action. Includes some facts. Fails to express his/her point of view. Does not compose or support a thesis statement. Does not use standard essay format (introduction, body, and conclusion). Writes less than 200 words or more than 300 words. Does not include a headline or the headline does not enhance the editorial.	Unable to begin effectively. Makes no attempt to begin an editorial.
Literacy: The Student Uses Knowledge of Nurturing to Write an Editorial	Collects and uses all facts learned from chapter 1 activities. Collects supporting information about nurturing from other sources. Shows an exceptional understanding of nurturing as a relationship and parenting skill.	Collects and uses all facts learned from chapter 1 activities. Shows high understanding of nurturing as a relationship and parenting skill.	Collects and uses most facts learned from chapter 1 activities. Shows understanding of nurturing as a relationship and parenting skill.	Does not use a complete and organized set of facts. Does not show understanding of nurturing.	Student begins but fails to complete an editorial. Unable to begin effectively. Makes no attempt to begin an editorial.

HANDOUT 11

Portfolio Project

PERIOD _____ NAME _____

Reading *Kids Today, Parents Tomorrow* will help you grow as a person. You will gain a greater understanding of the dynamics of relationships, especially between parent and child. The knowledge and skills you receive from this program can improve your relationships today and can prepare you for your tomorrows. Tomorrow may see you struggling to complete college, a day's work outside the home, or your eighth diaper change of the day!

A portfolio is a great way to take this knowledge beyond the classroom. Portfolio pieces can be used for peer education, academic competitions, or for publicity at school or in the community. A portfolio is impressive when shown during a job interview. Knowing how to compile a portfolio is a skill that can help you in college or on the job. Someday, your portfolio may be the right place to find answers to your parenting questions.

From a teacher's point of view, a portfolio can show that you have mastered the content of *Kids Today, Parents Tomorrow*.

Chapter	Portfolio Content	Completed
Chapter 1	Nature/Nurture Display Editorial	_____ _____
Chapter 2	Instruction Pamphlet Persuasive Speech	_____ _____
Chapter 3	Listening Questionnaire	_____
Chapter 4	Grade Card	_____
Chapter 5	Bookmark	_____
Chapter 6	Japanese Notebook	_____

Chapter 7	Responsibility Chart	_____
Chapter 8	Decision Tree Business Card	_____
Chapter 9	Aztec Codex (Anger and Reducing Anger) Optional: Educational Video on Anger	_____ _____
Chapter 10	Essential Elephant Optional: Community Service Video	_____ _____
Chapter 11	Application for a Parenting License	_____

After completing the entire portfolio, you will receive a "Prepared for Parenthood" certificate. This certificate completes your portfolio.

HANDOUT 12

Essential Questions

PERIOD _____ NAME _____

1. As explained in the chapter, focusing on misbehavior is not an effective way to encourage children to behave better. What might be some outcomes of being critical (focusing on misbehavior) with children and in other relationships?

2. What can we do to encourage children to behave better?

3. What is reinforcement?

4. What is a reinforcer?

5. How does positive attention work as a reinforcer with adults and children? Give some examples of positive attention.

6. Does negative attention act as reinforcement? Give a few examples of negative attention.

7. What are the four steps to finding and reinforcing the good?

8. How do parents and children (and people in all kinds of relationships) benefit from finding and reinforcing the good behavior?

HANDOUT 13

Advice Column

PERIOD _____ NAME _____

Your local newspaper has a great advice columnist whose name is "Dear Pappy." "Dear Pappy's" specialty is parent-child relationships. Imagine you are a parent feeling some distress over your child's misbehavior. You decide to write a letter to "Dear Pappy."

Here's what you need to do to write your letter:

- Write on a piece of binder paper.

- Begin with "Dear Pappy."

- Give some background information about yourself, your child, the rest of your family, where you live, and so on. Include any pertinent information that might help "Dear Pappy" respond with appropriate advice.

- Explain the exact problem that is causing you distress.

- Your problem must be related to your inability to manage your child's misbehavior. Use the examples in chapter 2 for ideas. Keep in mind that the focus of the chapter is how to reinforce good behavior.

- Ask for advice.

- Sign off with a name that reflects your problem, for example, "Signed, Sleepless In Seattle."

Now, for the fun part . . .

When students' letters are completed, they are collected and randomly distributed to other class members.

You are now "Dear Pappy" and it's your job to write an answer to someone else's problem in your next advice column.

Include the following in your advice column response:

- Write on a piece of binder paper.

- Begin with "Dear _____" (Use the name the student used to sign off his or her letter.)

- Consider the background and family situation as you write your advice. Refer back to the information in chapter 2 to suggest ways that this parent can (1) manage the child's behavior and (2) help the child learn to manage his or her own behavior. Give the parent lots of information so that what you suggest will be clearly understood.

- Sign off "Signed, Dear Pappy."

HANDOUT 14

Five-Day Diary

PERIOD _____ NAME _____

Keep a diary for five days. The purpose of the diary is to make you aware of two things: 1) how frequently others reinforce your speech and behavior, and 2) how frequently you reinforce the speech and behavior of others.

Every time you are reinforced, briefly describe the situation. Every time you reinforce someone else, briefly describe the situation. Make note of both positive reinforcement or attention (praise, a smile, kind words) and negative reinforcement or attention (scolding, a frown).

Description of Reinforcement   **+? OR −?**

Day 1

_____

Day 2

_____

Day 3

_____

Day 4

_____

Day 5

HANDOUT 15

Instruction Pamphlet

PERIOD _____ NAME _____

You're the owner of a successful chain of restaurants. When you had two stores, you were able to train all the new employees yourself. You were a good trainer because the new employees responded quickly to your use of positive reinforcement instead of criticism. After you opened your third store, however, you turned over the training to the store managers. Now, the managers are complaining that they don't know how to train new employees, worker efficiency has dropped, and there is increasing employee turnover. Plans are underway to open a fourth store. You know that something has got to be done about new employee training.

After studying the issue, you discover that your managers are knowledgeable about store operations; however, they tend to use criticism to correct new employees' work habits. You decide to publish a little pamphlet to give to the store managers during a workshop on how to train employees. The purpose of the pamphlet is to encourage the managers to use positive reinforcement when they must give employees directions.

Fold your piece of 12" x 18" white paper once as shown. On the inside, draw bold lines to divide the space into four sections, using either a or b as your model.

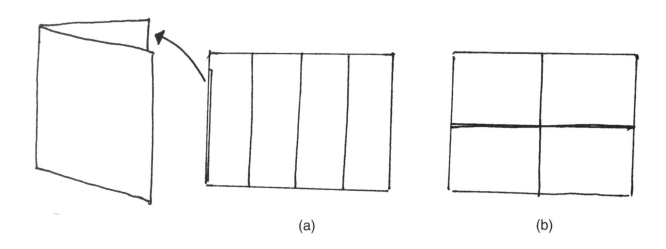

(a)   (b)

Your pamphlet needs to have the following elements:

The Cover Design

- The cover must show the title, *Four Steps to Guiding Employees*.

- Your restaurants are all named "The Panama Rainforest." The restaurants are decorated with pictures of Kuna Indian molas depicting natural, animal, and bird motifs. Make a construction paper mola for the cover of your pamphlet.

Directions:

1. Layer four or more different colors of 9" x 12" construction paper over the white cover of your pamphlet.

2. Draw the outline of an animal, bird, or other motif from nature on the top piece.

3. Cut through one layer at a time to create a multicolored design.

4. Glue the layers together.

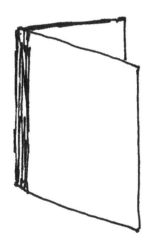

Content Inside Your Pamphlet

In the sections inside your pamphlet, write a summary of each of the four steps to finding and reinforcing the good. Remember to write in the context of a business relationship, not a parent-child relationship.

First Section: Step 1—**Ignore the Misbehavior**

Explain that it would be a better practice to state boundaries and redirect employee behaviors. Explain *why* it doesn't work to criticize misbehavior.

Second Section: Step 2—**Find Behaviors That You Feel OK About**

Suggest five desired work habits that the managers can look for and to which they can give positive reinforcement.

Third Section: Step 3—**Reinforce That Behavior with Positive Attention**

List at least ten ways that managers can give positive reinforcement.

Fourth Section: Step 4—**Gradually Start Reinforcing Only Those Behaviors You Want Repeated**

List the benefits of positive reinforcement for managers, employees, and the success of the business.

HANDOUT 16

Persuasive Speech

PERIOD _____ NAME _____

In two months you will open a fourth Panama Rainforest Restaurant. After the opening of the third store, you began to delegate extra duties to the restaurant managers. The only new duty that the managers have voiced concern about is training employees. They asked for your help. Everyone agrees that one big reason for your success is your ability to work with people, the natural ease with which you teach employees to provide excellent service.

You want to help your managers by giving them a few tips on training new employees, so you are offering a workshop, "Four Steps to Guiding Employees." All the planning and preparation is finished; you even published a pamphlet for the managers to use as a reference.

Now, the most difficult part of preparing for the workshop is your opening remarks. You want to clearly state the purpose for gathering everyone together; however, you do not want to appear to be critical of the way the managers have been dealing with employees in the recent past.

Follow these steps to write a short speech to open the workshop:

- Prewrite: *Gather facts* about finding and reinforcing the good. Use material from your chapter 2 reading and assignments.

- After reviewing the facts, decide your *point of view*. Point of view refers to your *opinion* on the practice of finding and reinforcing the good. You have already decided that your managers will be more effective at employee training if they practice the four steps to finding and reinforcing good behavior instead of focusing on misbehavior or criticism.

- Write a *thesis statement*. Your thesis statement tells the subject of your speech (reinforcing the good) and your point of view on the subject. A thesis statement appeals to the audience to do or to believe something. Your thesis statement needs to give an opinion that can be supported with sound reasoning and evidence.

- Remember your purpose for holding the workshop. The managers asked for your expert advice on how to train employees differently and better. The purpose of your speech is to justify using the four steps to find and reinforce good behavior and to convince the managers to follow the four steps. You want to avoid criticizing.

- Know your *audience*. The better you know your audience, the better you will be able to make arguments which will convince that audience. In this case, your audience is composed of your higher level employees.

- Follow the pattern of organization that you would use for an essay. In the *introduction* of your speech, introduce your point of view and your thesis statement. The *body* of your speech explains your point of view and presents reasons and evidence in support of your opinion. The *conclusion* summarizes the main points of your speech or restates the thesis statement in a new way.

- Your speech should be from *200 to 300 words long*, and run for two to three minutes.

- You must turn in a *typed* copy.

HANDOUT 17

Assessment Rubric for Pamphlet and Speech

PERIOD _____ NAME _____

_____ Check if complete

PAMPHLET (Teacher determines scores and/or grades)

Cover

Has a paper mola design _____

Has the title "Four Steps to Guiding Employees" _____

Inside section 1 contains:

Step 1 with an explanation _____

Explanation of why criticism doesn't work _____

Inside section 2 contains:

Step 2 with an explanation _____

Five desired work habits that the managers can look for _____

Inside section 3 contains:

Step 3 with an explanation _____

At least ten ways that managers can give positive attention _____

Inside section 4 contains:

Step 4 with an explanation _____

A list of the benefits of positive reinforcement for managers, employees, and the success of the business _____

_____ Check if complete

PERSUASIVE SPEECH

Point of view is clearly stated _____

Thesis statement is clearly stated _____

Your speech is tailored to the audience _____

The introduction of your speech contains your point of view and your thesis statement

_____

The body of your speech explains your point of view and presents reasons and evidence in support of your opinion _____

The conclusion summarizes your point of view and /or restates the thesis statement in a new way _____

Your speech is between 200 and 300 words long _____

You turned in a typed copy _____

COMMENTS

PAMPHLET SCORE/GRADE _____   **SPEECH SCORE/GRADE** _____

HANDOUT 18

Hello-O!?

Make one copy of these instruction cards for each group:

Volunteer Speaker

> Tell your group a little about your life.
>
> Tell your full name.
>
> Tell where you were born.
>
> Give the date of your birth.
>
> Describe your family (give names of family members and ages of brothers and sisters).
>
> Tell your favorite memory from your childhood.
>
> Tell the names of the elementary and middle schools you attended.
>
> Tell the names of one or two favorite teachers from the past and why they were your favorites.
>
> Tell your current grade in school.
>
> Name your favorite subjects.
>
> Tell a little about your best friends.

-- CUT --

"Listener" Stay seated in the circle.

Do the following while the volunteer is talking:

Listen for the first forty seconds (count to forty in your head) and then ignore the speaker for the rest of the time by talking to the person next to you.

-- CUT --

"Listener" Stay seated in the circle.

Do the following while the volunteer is talking:

Listen for the first forty seconds (count to forty in your head) and then ignore the speaker for the rest of the time by daydreaming and looking away from the speaker.

-- CUT --

"Listener" Stay seated in the circle.

Do the following while the volunteer is talking:

Listen for the first forty seconds (count to forty in your head) and then ignore the speaker for the rest of the time by closing your eyes and taking a rest.

-- CUT --

"Listener" Stay seated in the circle.

Do the following while the volunteer is talking:

Listen for the first forty seconds (count to forty in your head) and then ignore the speaker for the rest of the time by gazing at and pretending to be fixing your fingernails.

-- CUT --

"Listener" Stay seated in the circle.

Do the following while the volunteer is talking:

Listen for the first forty seconds (count to forty in your head) and then ignore the speaker for the rest of the time by practicing your karate moves.

-- CUT --

HANDOUT 19

Mind-Map Mobile

PERIOD _____ NAME _____

A mind map is just another way to organize the chapter information mind map with either words, take notes. During or after reading chapter 3, using the organizer below. You may fill in the symbols, or pictures.

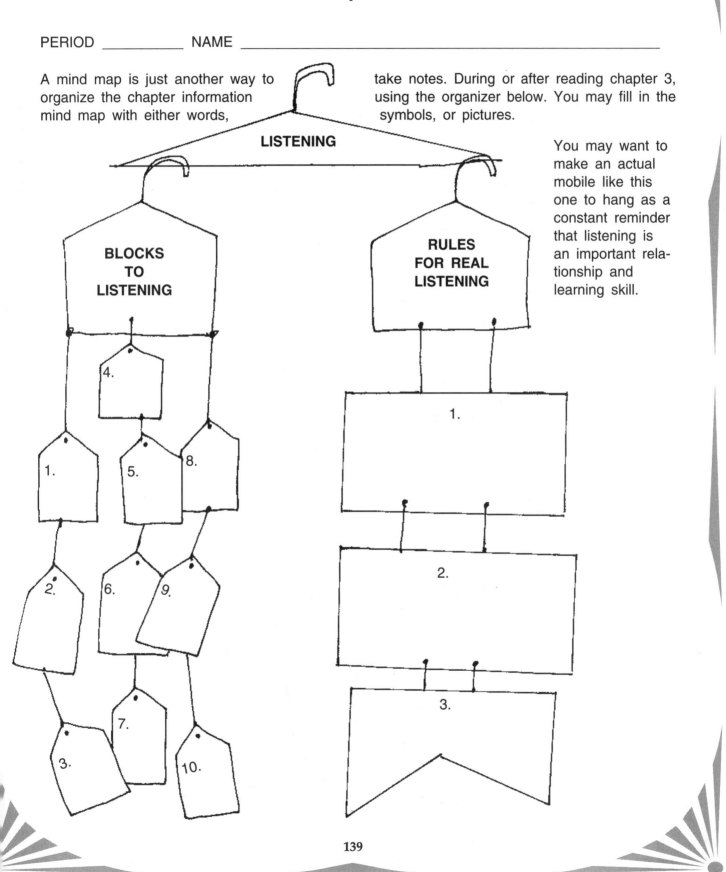

You may want to make an actual mobile like this one to hang as a constant reminder that listening is an important relationship and learning skill.

HANDOUT 20

Essential Questions

PERIOD _____ NAME _____

1. Why is listening an important relationship skill?

2. What is the difference between pseudo listening and real listening?

3. Give a brief explanation of how each of the following "blocks to listening" inhibits the listener's ability to really listen:

   - Mind-reading

   - Rehearsing

   - Filtering

   - Judging

   - Daydreaming

   - Advising

   - Sparring

   - Being right

- Derailing

- Placating

4. What might be some outcomes of not listening to children and others?

5. What are the three steps or rules to good listening?

(1)

(2)

(3)

What are some ways you can show with your body that you are listening?

As an active listener, what can you do or say to increase your understanding of what the speaker is experiencing and feeling?

How is paraphrasing done?

What is feedback and how does one give feedback?

6. How do individuals benefit and relationships improve when there is real listening?

HANDOUT 21

Listening Crossword

Use the clues given to fill in the crossword puzzle. All clues and words are taken from chapter 3 and are related to listening skills.

DOWN

1. Saying in your own words what you've heard the other person say.

2. When you tell the person your reaction to what he or she has said, you are giving _____ .

3. A pseudo listener does this when he or she offers what they think to be the perfect solution.

4. This means that a psuedo listener will go to any lengths to avoid the suggestion that he or she is wrong.

5. This kind of listening occurs when the listener's intention is to "pass" for listening instead of really listening.

6. _____ involves tuning out certain topics, hearing only what one wants to hear.

7. This block to listening involves listening only enough to find something to disagree with.

8. When a listener decides ahead of time that the other person is bad, and, therefore, only listens for evidence to confirm that opinion.

9. In an attempt to be nice or to be liked, a listener agrees with everything being said without really listening.

10. Paying half attention to the person talking, while allowing one's thoughts to wander.

11. Maintaining _____ contributes to listening with full attention.

ACROSS

1. Instead of listening, the listener plans out in her head what she is going to say next.

2. This is done when a listener pays more attention to what he thinks the person "really means" instead of what the person is really saying.

3. This kind of listening implies that you want to understand what the other person is saying, thinking, feeling, and needing.

4. This occurs when the listener changes the subject or jokes when she becomes bored or uncomfortable with the conversation.

5. The second step to good listening is attending to the _____ being conveyed as well as to the content of the message.

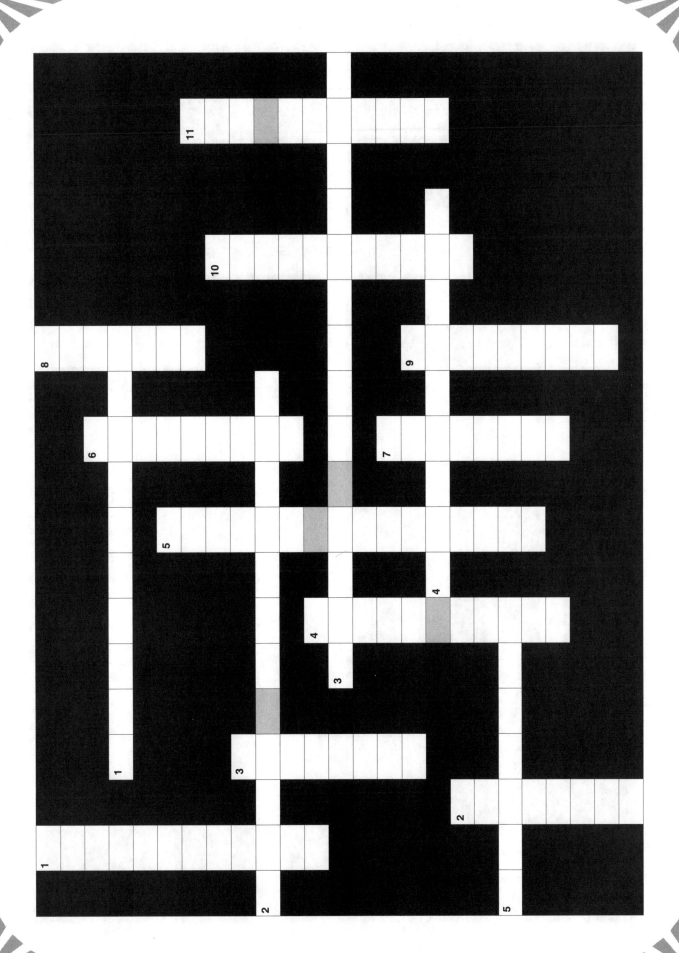

143

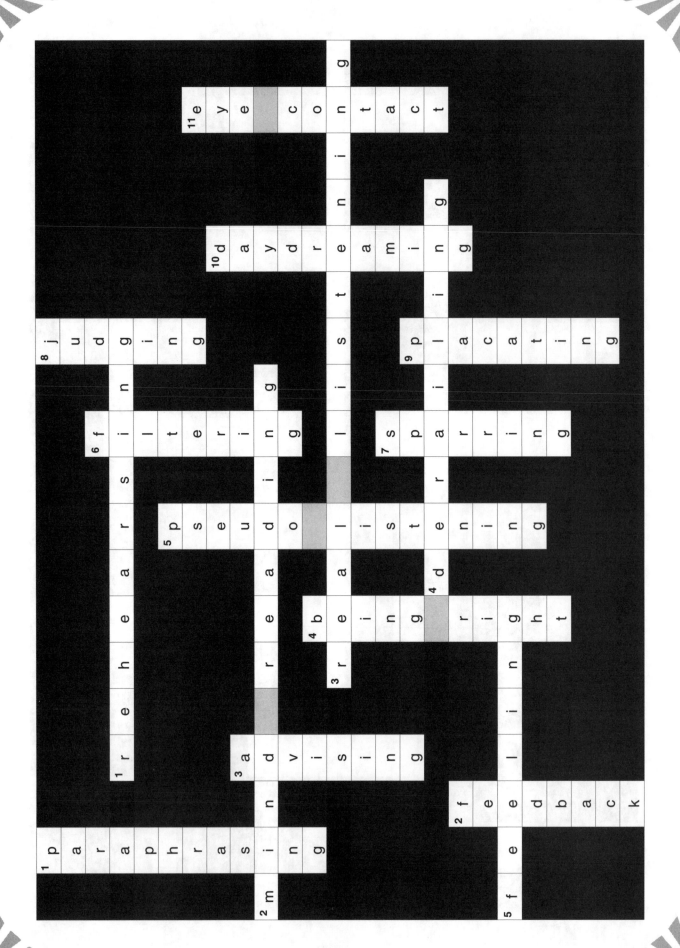

HANDOUT 22

Data Collection Sheet—Time Spent Listening

PERIOD _____ NAME _____

Fill in the chart as you go through a typical twenty-four hour "school day." Use pencil or gray to shade in the time slots spent in the act of listening (to anyone or anything). Put an asterisk (*) in the gray shaded boxes when you spend most of that time slot in **real listening**. Use blue to shade in the time slots spent in all the activities that do not require any listening at all. Use red to shade in the time spent sleeping. Use ink pen and pencil and/or felt-tipped pens and crayons. Begin at whatever time you receive this sheet. Each line represents a ten-minute time slot.

6:00 a.m. _____	12:00 noon _____	6:00 p.m. _____	12:00 midnight _____
10 _____	10 _____	10 _____	10 _____
20 _____	20 _____	20 _____	20 _____
30 _____	30 _____	30 _____	30 _____
40 _____	40 _____	40 _____	40 _____
50 _____	50 _____	50 _____	50 _____
7:00 _____	1:00 _____	7:00 _____	1:00 _____
10 _____	10 _____	10 _____	10 _____
20 _____	20 _____	20 _____	20 _____
30 _____	30 _____	30 _____	30 _____
40 _____	40 _____	40 _____	40 _____
50 _____	50 _____	50 _____	50 _____
8:00 _____	2:00 _____	8:00 _____	2:00 _____
10 _____	10 _____	10 _____	10 _____
20 _____	20 _____	20 _____	20 _____
30 _____	30 _____	30 _____	30 _____
40 _____	40 _____	40 _____	40 _____
50 _____	50 _____	50 _____	50 _____
9:00 _____	3:00 _____	9:00 _____	3:00 _____
10 _____	10 _____	10 _____	10 _____
20 _____	20 _____	20 _____	20 _____
30 _____	30 _____	30 _____	30 _____
40 _____	40 _____	40 _____	40 _____
50 _____	50 _____	50 _____	50 _____
10:00 _____	4:00 _____	10:00 _____	4:00 _____
10 _____	10 _____	10 _____	10 _____
20 _____	20 _____	20 _____	20 _____
30 _____	30 _____	30 _____	30 _____
40 _____	40 _____	40 _____	40 _____
50 _____	50 _____	50 _____	50 _____
11:00 _____	5:00 _____	11:00 _____	5:00 _____
10 _____	10 _____	10 _____	10 _____
20 _____	20 _____	20 _____	20 _____
30 _____	30 _____	30 _____	30 _____
40 _____	40 _____	40 _____	40 _____
50 _____	50 _____	50 _____	50 _____

HANDOUT 23

Listening Pie

PERIOD _____ NAME _____

If I said, "Listening is a critical relationship skill," would you believe me? Everyone seems to agree that good communication is the most important aspect of any relationship; however, few people ever stop and actually think about what constitutes effective communication and why it is so important. The goal of this activity is to get you to realize the amount of time you spend listening, and, therefore, that listening has a huge impact on the quality and success of your relationships.

Organize the data you collected on Handout 22.

Gray = Time spent listening

_____ Hours and _____ Minutes

* (asterisk) = Time spent in **real listening**

_____ Hours and _____ Minutes

Blue = Time spent in activities that do not require listening

_____ Hours and _____ Minutes

Red = Time spent sleeping

_____ Hours and _____ Minutes

Make a pie graph (also known as a circle graph) to show what percent of your day is spent in each of the activities above:

STEP 1. The total number of hours in a day is 24. Your whole pie graph will represent 24 hours.

STEP 2. Express the data in whole hours and fractions of an hour, using decimals.

10 Minutes = .16 of an hour

20 Minutes = .33 of an hour

30 Minutes = .50 of an hour

40 Minutes = .66 of an hour

50 Minutes = .83 of an hour

Gray _____ . _____ hours

* _____ . _____ hours

Blue _____ . _____ hours

Red _____ . _____ hours

STEP 3. To determine the portion of the day spent in each activity, divide the number of hours spent in each activity (Step No. 2) by the total number of hours in a day (Step No. 1). **Example:** If there are 24 hours in a day and 16 of them were spent listening (gray), you would divide 16 by 24 (16 ÷ 24 = 0.166666 . . .). Round off to the nearest hundredth and express as a percent by moving the decimal point two places to the right and adding the percent (%) sign. **Example:** 67%.

Gray _____ ÷ 24 = 0. _____ OR _____ %

*   _____ ÷ 24 = 0. _____ OR _____ %

Blue _____ ÷ 24 = 0. _____ OR _____ %

Red _____ ÷ 24 = 0. _____ OR _____ %

STEP 4. To determine the size of each section of the pie graph (the size of each central angle), write each percent as a decimal and multiply by 360. Round the answers to the nearest degree.

Example: 0.67 x 360 = 241.20 (241°).

Gray 0. _____ x 360° = _____ °

*   0. _____ x 360° = _____ °

Blue 0. _____ x 360° = _____ °

Red 0. _____ x 360° = _____ °

STEP 5. Line up the center of the protractor (◠) with the center of the circle, placing the straight edge of the protractor on the given radius. Find and mark the central angle for gray (portion of day spent listening) along the curved edge of the protractor; begin at 0 and follow the curve until you find the degree of angle for which you are looking. Use a ruler to draw a line from the center of the circle to mark the point on the edge of the circle. Color this piece of the pie gray and label it, "Percentage of Time Spent Listening." Repeat for blue (portion of day spent in activities not requiring listening) and red (portion of day spent sleeping), using the edge of the last piece of the pie as the new radius.

Example: If a 241° angle is needed to show that 67% of the day is spent listening, you would need to go 61° beyond 180°.

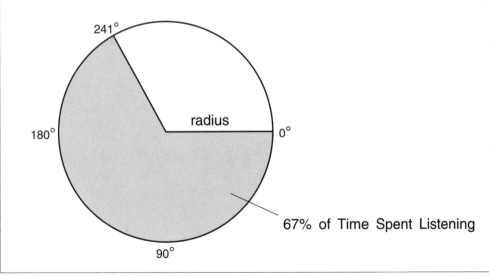

Draw, label, and color the gray, blue, and red pieces of your pie graph:

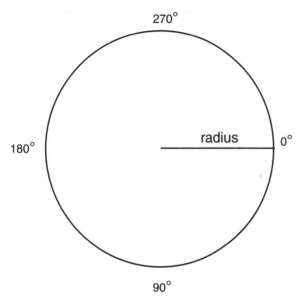

STEP 6. Follow the instructions under Step 5 to make an overlay on top of the gray pie piece (time spent in listening). This will show the portion of time you were engaged in **real listening (*)** out of the total time spent listening. Use a pencil to make darker cross-hatching over the gray to show the amount of time you spent in real listening.

Example: If 4 hours (17%) of your day was spent in <u>real listening</u>, you would draw a 61° angled piece of pie over the gray area (.17 x 360 = 61.20 or 61°).

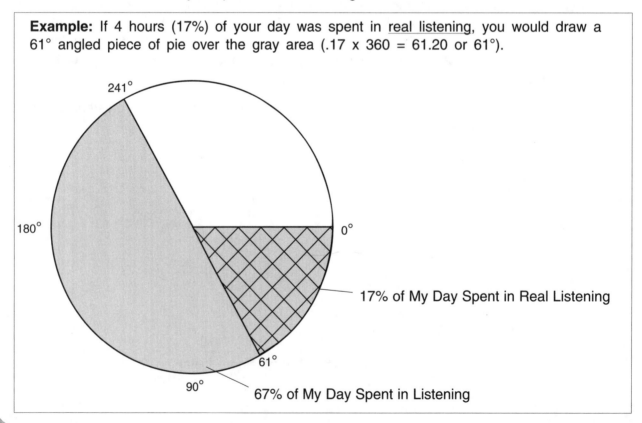

HANDOUT 24

Side 1

empathy

Empathy is one way that listeners attend to the feelings as well as the content of the message. Listeners put themselves in the other person's shoes and try to know that person's feelings. This can be achieved when the listener reads the other person's facial expression, tone of voice, body posture, etc. Also, by the listener trying to imagine how it would feel to be in a similar situation.

Hold up this card every time you think the listener (the sandwich maker) is using empathy to attend to the feelings as well as the content of the message.

Chapter 3

HANDOUT 25

Side 1

clarification

Clarification: The listener asks clarifying questions to get more information in order to understand and acknowledge what the other person is saying.

Hold up this card every time you hear the listener (the sandwich maker) ask a clarifying question.

Chapter 3

HANDOUT 26

Side 1

paraphrasing

Paraphrasing: A listener uses paraphrasing to let a speaker know that both the content and the feelings which were expressed have been heard. A listener paraphrases by saying in his or her own words what the other person was heard to say, for example, "It sounds like you're really frustrated by these instructions and you're also worried that we won't be able to make your sandwich."

Hold up this card every time the listener (the sandwich maker) paraphrases.

Chapter 3

HANDOUT 27

Side 1

feedback

Feedback: After listeners have heard and acknowledged what the other person has said, they sometimes give feedback. The listener gives feedback by <u>telling the other person his or her reaction</u> to what they've heard. For example, the listener might say, "So, we both agree that we should spread the peanut butter with the knife."

Hold up this card every time you hear the listener (the sandwich maker) give feedback.

Chapter 3

HANDOUT 28

Listening Questionnaire

PERIOD _____ NAME _____

Think of all the questionnaires you have seen in teen magazines. They are fun to fill out, they are informative, and they do tell you something about your own relationship skills.

This is your chance to be a staff writer for *Magazine X*, the most popular teen magazine on the planet! Your editor, who calls herself Xena the Publishing Warrior (XPW), has decided that the back-to-school issue will be devoted to helping teens build better relationships. She wants the focus to be on interpersonal communication skills: self-expression and listening. XPW has recognized that you have excellent communication skills, especially when it comes to listening to co-workers and friends. She has asked you to write the feature article and questionnaire on **real listening**. Your article (which you don't actually write) would probably contain the same information, ideas, and tips as chapter 3 of *Kids Today, Parents Tomorrow*.

Your assignment is to develop a questionnaire that your readers could complete before reading your article. The purpose of the questionnaire is to assess the reader's current skill as a listener and make him or her aware of the importance of real listening in relationships. This questionnaire can also make the reader aware that pseudo listening is common. **Real listening**, however, can be mastered if your article is read and the listening skills are practiced! Quite often, questionnaires have been shown to motivate readers to read articles, especially if they receive a low score!

Assignment Instructions:

(1) Using twenty questions or less, your questionnaire must include the main concepts about pseudo listening and **real listening** from chapter 3. Refer back to your chapter notes, essential questions/answers, and assignment handouts. Each question should examine the reader's knowledge of or ability related to one concept or skill.

Example:

Do you find yourself changing the subject or joking around whenever you become bored or uncomfortable with a conversation?

    a. Often

    b. Never

    c. Sometimes

This question relates to "derailing," which is a block to real listening.

---

(2). You can develop any type of scoring system for the answers. Most questionnaires assign a point value for each response related to the person's knowledge of the topic, in this case, listening.

Example: How You Rate as a Listener

Give yourself 0 points for every "a" answer; 10 points for every "b" answer; and 5 points for every "c" answer.

---

(3). Write a profile describing the knowledge and ability level for each point range.

Example:

If you scored between 40 and 60, you are a **real listener**, which means you practice listening.

HANDOUT 29

Make a Mask

PERIOD _____ NAME _____

Chapter 4

HANDOUT 30

Essential Questions

PERIOD _____ NAME _____

1. Why is it important to express yourself?

2. What are the three steps in expressing yourself? (Give a brief explanation of each.)

    (1)

    (2)

    (3)

3. What are some tips for better self-expression? (Give a brief explanation of each.)

    *

    *

    *

    *

    *

4. What are some communication habits that interfere with self-expression and should be avoided?

    *

    *

    *

    *

    *

    *

    *

    *

    *

    *

Chapter 4

HANDOUT 31

Three-Step Express Yourself Exercise

PERIOD _____ NAME _____

It is important to express yourself in the most useful and healthy way. Listed below are some statements that might be offensive instead of expressive. Follow the three steps in expressing yourself to change these statements so that they are more likely to be heard and to engage the cooperation of others.

"I hate it when you leave your shoes on the bathroom floor!"

> **Example:** *Your shoes are on the floor. I feel frustrated when I have to walk over them. I want you to take them off in your bedroom and store them in your closet.*

_____

A. "If you don't pick up your toys, I'll throw them in the trash."

_____

B. "You talk too much! Leave me alone so I can do my homework."

_____

C. "A true friend should be there for me when I go into the hospital."

_____

D. "You are always late! I never know what to expect. I never know when to be ready."

_____

E. "Don't yell at me. You weren't paying attention to what was really happening. I was trying to get them to settle down and follow the rules."

_____

F. "Yuk! I want to run away whenever you try to buy clothes for me! It's so embarrassing!"

_____

HANDOUT 32

Diagramming

PERIOD _____ NAME _____

This can be a fun way to check the effectiveness of the expressions you wrote on Handout 31. Pick four of the expressions you wrote, separate the three parts of the expression, and "plug" the parts into the diagrams provided. If your expressions included all three steps required to express yourself, then you have some winners!

Example: Offensive Statement. "I hate it when you leave your shoes on the bathroom floor."

Example: More Expressive Statement. "Your shoes are on the floor. I feel frustrated when I have to step over them. I want you to take them off in your bedroom and store them in the closet."

1. *Your shoes are on the floor.* _____

1. Describes the situation.

2. *I feel frustrated when I have to step over them.* _____

2. Uses an "I" statement to describe feelings.

3. *I want you to take them off in your bedroom and store them in the closet.* _____

3. Describes what is wanted or needed in the situation.

_____

Expression 1:

1. _____

1. Describes the situation.

2. _____

2. Uses an "I" statement to describe feelings.

3. _____

3. Describes what is wanted or needed in the situation.

Expression 2:

1. _____

1. Describes the situation.

2. _____

2. Uses an "I" statement to describe feelings.

3. _____

3. Describes what is wanted or needed in the situation.

Expression 3:

1. _____

1. Describes the situation.

2. _____

2. Uses an "I" statement to describe feelings.

3. _____

3. Describes what is wanted or needed in the situation.

Expression 4:

1. _____

1. Describes the situation.

2. _____

2. Uses an "I" statement to describe feelings.

3. _____

3. Describes what is wanted or needed in the situation.

Chapter 4

HANDOUT 33

Imagine (Free Write)

PERIOD _____ NAME _____

Chapter 4 showed us that expressing ourselves is the way we convey what we want, our likes and dislikes, our thoughts, feelings, opinions, reactions, and decisions and also the way we get our needs met. In this chapter we learned three steps to effective self-expression. Effective self-expression is more likely to be heard and to engage the cooperation of others than other forms of communication. Chapter 4 also explained why the "do's" work and the "don'ts" don't!

I am sure we are all more aware of what works and we all try to express ourselves in more useful ways.

Well, what if we succeeded? What if all the people in our school began to follow the directions in chapter 4 and expressed themselves effectively every time? How would that change the culture* of our school?

Do a free write on lined paper. Ponder this idea, considering the ideas expressed in the first paragraph above. In what ways would individuals change? How would our thoughts, speech, and actions change? Would our beliefs change? How about our social groups? Would this change our interactions? Would we teach and learn differently? Include in your writing answers to these questions: "Would you be happy with the changes? Why? Why not?"

* Here, *culture* means the customary beliefs, social forms, and material traits of a social group.

Staple your free write to this Handout when you turn it in.

HANDOUT 34

Grade Card

PERIOD _____ NAME _____

After reading and studying chapter 4 are you better at expressing yourself? We all know that communication skills must be practiced to be perfected.

Create a grade card for your portfolio that will help you remember the three steps in expressing yourself and the "do's" and "don'ts" of expressing yourself. Pretend that this grade card will be used to evaluate statements made by people who are trying to express themselves in a relationship situation. Your grade card must include the *specifics* of the following criteria for effective expression:

Three Steps in Expressing Yourself

The "Do's" for Better Self Expression

The "Don'ts": Habits That Interfere with Self-Expression

Is the expression likely to get the speaker what he or she needs or wants?

Is the expression likely to engage the cooperation of others?

Did the expression convey likes, dislikes, thoughts, feelings, opinions, reactions, or decisions?

Your grade card must present all of the above as a checklist and must show a numerical or lettered rating system for each criterion.

You can title and decorate your grade card in any way you choose.

Example:

Criteria for Effective Self-Expression	Observations	Rating 0 = Not Achieved 5 = Achieved
Did the speaker use the three-steps in expressing himself or herself?	Describe the situation? Yes No Use "I" message? Yes No Describe what he wants/needs? Yes No	
Was the speaker . . .	clear honest consistent immediate supportive appropriate (circle)	
Did the speaker avoid the "don'ts"?	judging labeling lecturing/moralizing commanding threatening comparisons (cross out the ones not used)	

Criteria for Effective Self-Expression	Observations	Rating 0 = Not Achieved 5 = Achieved

HANDOUT 35

Idea Clouds

PERIOD _____ NAME _____

As you read chapter 5, write the main ideas on different clouds. Use as many clouds as you need. Draw more clouds if you need them!

WHOSE PROBLEM IS IT?

HANDOUT 36

Puzzled About Who Owns the Problem?

PERIOD _____ NAME _____

Cut out the shapes on page 2 of Handout 36 and glue them in place on this page. Place them in what would be the most logical sequence of events.

You now know what communication skill to use in seeking a solution to the problem.

Be an active listener.

You ask . . . whose rights or needs are being thwarted?

Express yourself

Do nothing

There is a problem.

You own the problem.

Both own the problem.

The other person owns the problem.

You need to determine who owns the problem.

There's no problem

Listen <u>and</u> express yourself.

HANDOUT 37

A Gift—Part 1

PERIOD _____ NAME _____

One meaning of the word "gift" is to endow with some power, quality, or attribute. In this activity you will make a gift for one of your friends or relatives. Hopefully, this gift will endow that friend or relative with the power to determine who owns the problem, a critical skill in interpersonal communication.

Your gift is a guide containing instructions for determining who owns the problem. Pass on the instructions that you learned from chapter 5 activities.

Your guide must be made in the form of a bookmark. Yes, it will be possible to fit all the necessary instructions on a bookmark! Your assignment is to make two beautiful keepsake bookmarks, one to give and one to keep. The one you keep will become part of your portfolio.

All materials needed to make and decorate the bookmarks will be provided. The pattern and instructions for making the bookmark are on page 2 of this Handout. The instructions for determining who owns the problem need to be neatly printed by hand directly onto the stiff bookmark base or typed, cut out, and glued onto the bookmark base.

Example:

Whose Problem Is It?

To determine who owns the problem ask yourself: Whose rights are being violated? OR Whose needs are not being met?

Based on who owns the problem, respond in the following ways:

If you own the problem express yourself using an I message and/or use your problem solving skills.

If the other person owns the problem, be an active listener.

If both people own the problem, both need to use their skills to solve the problem.

If there's no problem, you need not be involved.

"E Pluribus Unum"—Part 2

e plu-ri-bus u-num [Latin]: one out of many—used on the seal of the United States and on several U.S. coins

Before reading chapter 5, you probably didn't think about the many times in each day you are involved in various types of problem situations . . . the many times you are required to express yourself or to really listen in important situations with friends and family. You might have been surprised to learn that knowing who owns the problem is necessary before you can know what your responsibility is in a relationship and which communication skill to use.

For one whole day be aware of all the times you are involved in situations that require you to assess who owns the problem. Pick *one out of the many,* and then write a report describing the situation: (1) Who owned the problem? (2) How did you determine who owned the problem? and (3) How did the people who engaged in communication settle the issue? This report will go into your portfolio with the bookmark guide. Attach your report to this sheet with the bookmark when you turn it in.

Instructions for Making Two Keepsake Bookmarks

1. Cut out the pattern. Trace it twice onto stiff paper. Cut out each bookmark base.

2. Punch a hole in the top of each bookmark. Look at the example on page 1.

3. Neatly print (or type, cut out, and glue on) the instructions for determining who owns the problem on one side of each bookmark. It should look something like the example on the previous page.

4. Decorate both sides of both bookmarks.

5. Laminate both bookmarks or cover both sides of each with clear contact paper. You may need to repunch the hole.

6. For each bookmark, cut one to five strands of string about 16 inches long; thread the strings through the holes; decorate them further with knots and beads.

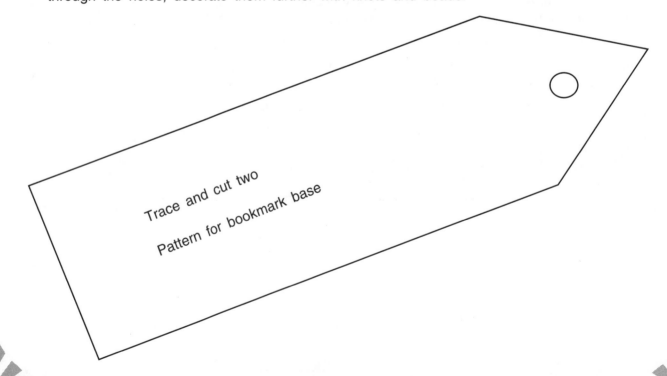

Trace and cut two

Pattern for bookmark base

Chapter 6

HANDOUT 38

Japanese Notebook

PERIOD _____ NAME _____

Follow the instructions to make a Japanese notebook.

1. Gather supplies:

    Four pieces of 8½" x 11" plain paper

    Two pieces of 8½" x 14" plain paper

    Two pieces of thin cardboard, each measuring 9½" x 6½"

    One piece of string about 16" long

    Two pieces of decorative paper measuring 8½" x 11½" and two pieces measuring 5½" x 8½"

2. Fold the four pieces of 8½" x 11" paper:

    Fold each in half crosswise. Folded papers will measure 5½" x 8½" These will be the inner pages (a) of your booklet.

3. Fold two pieces of 8 1/2" x 14" paper:

    Make two crosswise folds in each piece of paper, one at 5½" and one at 11".

    These will be the first and last pages (b) because they will each have an extra leaf to glue to the front and back covers of the booklet.

Here's what you should have at this point:

4. Glue the two pieces of decorative paper to the two pieces of thin cardboard, trimming off the corners and folding it around the cardboard as shown. These are the front and back covers of the booklet.

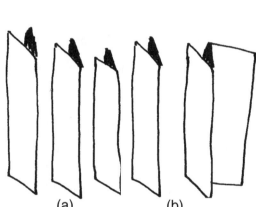

(b)   (a)   (b)

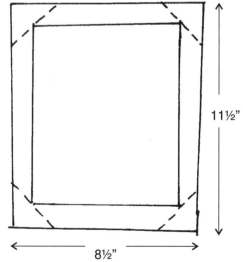

11½"

8½"

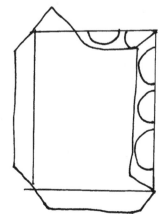

5. (1) Glue the short leaf of the 8½" x 14" first and last pages to the front and back covers of the booklet. (2) Glue the two pieces of 5½" x 8½" decorative paper over the leaf to finish the inside of each cover.

(1)

(2)

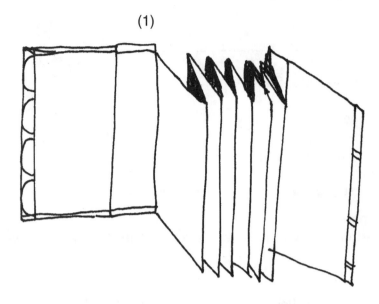
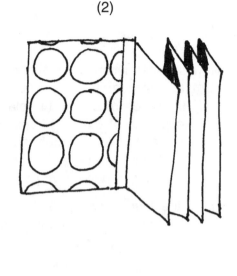

6. Punch two holes ½" in from the spine of the book, one located two inches down from the top and one located two inches up from the bottom. The hole punching must be done in three steps: (1) Punch the front cover first. (2) Mark the pages through the holes in the cover with a pencil, and punch all the pages at once. (3) Mark and punch the back cover. (4) Thread the string through the holes and tie it with a bow knot.

7. Fill in the pages with information you learned from chapter 6 as follows:

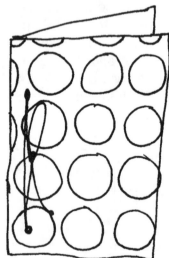

Page 1: Title, "The Five-Step Approach to Problem Solving"

Page 2: An Illustration (The illustrations can be anything you choose, your own drawings or photos, pictures cut out of magazines, drawings done by a friend, and so forth.)

Page 3: Step 1—Description and a Summary of That Step

Page 4: An Illustration

Page 5: Step 2—Description and a Summary of That Step

Page 6: An Illustration

Page 7: Step 3—Description and a Summary of That Step

Page 8: An Illustration

Page 9: Step 4—Description and a Summary of That Step

Page 10: An Illustration

Page 11: Step 5—Description and a Summary of That Step

HANDOUT 39

Five-Step Problem-Solving Process

DEFINE THE PROBLEM IN TERMS OF CONFLICTING NEEDS

BRAINSTORM POSSIBLE SOLUTIONS

EVALUATE AND ELIMINATE ALTERNATIVES

PICK THE BEST SOLUTION AND DEVELOP A PLAN

EVALUATE

HANDOUT 40

Three Steps in Expressing Yourself

DESCRIBE THE SITUATION

THEN SAY WHY THE SITUATION IS A PROBLEM FOR YOU

USE AN "I" STATEMENT TO DESCRIBE YOUR FEELINGS

DESCRIBE WHAT YOU WANT OR NEED IN THE SITUATION

HANDOUT 41

Five-Step or Express Yourself?

PERIOD _____ NAME _____

Whenever people get together (in the family, at school, at work, etc.) there will be inevitable conflicts of need. When you own any part of a problem, you can express yourself and/or use the five-step problem-solving process to seek a solution. Obviously, expressing yourself and listening are necessary anytime you want to cooperate with another person. The five-step approach to problem solving is effective in some situations and not in others. Can you recognize situations that call for the use of the five-step process?

Put a circle around the numbers of the situations that call for the five-step process and draw a square around the numbers of the situations that would be handled more effectively by expressing yourself and listening. For each choice, explain <u>why</u> you think that is the correct choice.

1. A family of four wants to go on a one-week vacation this summer. Everyone wants to do something different. Arguments are beginning to take place.

    Why?

2. Your brother took your new CD to a party. He returned it scratched and it seems to be skipping. You played it only once.

    Why?

3. You and another student are partners for an English class assignment. Both of you are willing to work on the project, but you haven't been able to schedule time to work together. You must get this project done in the next week in order to do your oral presentation before the deadline.

    Why?

4. You and another student are partners for an English class assignment. Every time you try to schedule a work time with the other person, that person says he/she can't make it. You're beginning to get worried because the deadline for oral reports is one week away.

    Why?

5. There is only one telephone line in your household. Your Dad and Mom have begun to trade stocks over the Internet and they spend about two hours online every night. All your friends are saying that they can never get through to you when they call. Your parents recognize the problem and are willing to work on a solution.

    Why?

6. Jessica's sister borrowed her new dress. When she took it out of the closet to wear to school, she noticed a stain on the front.

    Why?

7. Your parents are asking you to hurry up and decide which college you want to go to so that they can make some financial arrangements.

    Why?

PERIOD _____ NAME _____

Whenever people get together (in the family, at school, at work, etc.) there will be inevitable conflicts of need. When you own any part of a problem, you can express yourself and/or use the five-step problem-solving process to seek a solution. Obviously, expressing yourself and listening are necessary anytime you want to cooperate with another person. The five-step approach to problem solving is effective in some situations and not in others. Can you recognize situations that call for the use of the five-step process?

Put a circle around the number of the situations that call for the five-step process and draw a square around the numbers of the situations that would be handled more effectively by expressing yourself and listening. For each choice, explain <u>why</u> you think that is the correct choice.

1. A family of four wants to go on a one week vacation this summer. Everyone wants to do something different. Arguments are beginning to take place.

    Why? This family is experiencing a conflict of needs.

2. Your brother took your new CD to a party. He returned it scratched and it seems to be skipping. You only played it once.

    Why? There is no conflict of needs. You own the problem. You need to express yourself.

3. You and another student are partners for an English class assignment. Both of you are willing to work on the project, but you haven't been able to schedule time to work together. You must get this project done in the next week in order to do your oral presentation before the deadline.

    Why? Both partners are willing, but there is a conflict of needs because they haven't been able to manage their time to fit in working on the project.

4. You and another student are partners for an English class assignment. Every time you try to schedule a work time with the other person, that person says he/she can't make it. You're beginning to get worried because the deadline for oral reports is one week away.

    Why? There is no conflict of needs, because one partner is unwilling. In other words, that person doesn't feel the need to do the project. You own the problem and need to express yourself.

5. There is only one telephone line in your household. Your Dad and Mom have begun to trade stocks over the Internet and they spend about two hours online every night. All your friends are saying that they can never get through to you when they call. Your parents recognize the problem and are willing to work on a solution.

    Why? Both parties are willing to work out this conflict of needs.

6. Jessica's sister borrowed her new dress. When she took it out of the closet to wear to school, she noticed a stain on the front.

    Why? Jessica owns this problem and needs to express herself. There is no conflict of needs.

7. Your parents are asking you to hurry up and decide which college you want to go to so that they can make some financial arrangements.

    Why? There is a conflict of needs here.

Chapter 6

HANDOUT 42

For "A Teams"—Product Failure

PERIOD _____ NAMES _____ & _____

A TEAM: The two of you are recent college graduates who have just been hired by a well-known toy manufacturer. You were hired to form the new Problem-Solving Team. The company recently discovered that individual departments, such as Research and Development, Product Testing, Production, and Marketing, were wasting time in disagreements over problems and, in most cases, there was materials waste and lost profit.

Your team will work with other teams throughout the company whenever they have a problem. It will be your job to facilitate the problem-solving process. Therefore, you must be experts in the five-step problem-solving process and be able to guide other teams through the process efficiently.

Management has asked you, the Problem-Solving Team, to facilitate solving the problem of what to do with two million pounds of glow-in-the-dark playdough that comes in four colors. It can't be sold as playdough because it stains hands and clothing. If you dispose of the product, your company will suffer a huge financial loss. You will be working with a two-person team from the Production Department.

Refer back to the summaries in your Japanese notebook as you go through the following steps with the other team:

STEP 1—DEFINE THE PROBLEM (IN TERMS OF CONFLICTING NEEDS)

_____

_____

_____

_____

_____

STEP 2—BRAINSTORM POSSIBLE SOLUTIONS

_____

_____

_____

_____

_____

STEP 3—EVALUATE AND ELIMINATE ALTERNATIVES

Read each item on your list. Discuss each and cross off the suggestions that won't work. Eliminate those that anyone finds unacceptable.

STEP 4—PICK THE BEST SOLUTION AND DEVELOP A PLAN

The one possible solution that would work for all of you: _____

_____

_____

_____

_____

_____

_____

A detailed plan for putting that option into effect, including what each of you is going to do and when:

_____

_____

_____

_____

_____

_____

_____

When are you going to evaluate your plan and how will you decide if it's working or not?

_____

_____

_____

_____

_____

_____

STEP 5—EVALUATION: Evaluation can't be completed in this activity.

HANDOUT 42

For "B Teams"—Product Failure

PERIOD _____ NAMES _____ & _____

B TEAM: The two of you work in the Production Department of the same well-known toy manufacturer.

You received specifications for a new product, which included an order to produce two million pounds of the new product. The product is a glow-in-the-dark playdough that comes in four colors. The order was accompanied by a memo instructing you not to begin production until the completion of the last phase of product testing. Somehow, that memo was lost and your department went ahead with the production.

The last phase of product testing showed that the glow-in-the-dark colors stain hands and clothing. The lab people say they will make the necessary changes in the formulation for future production.

If you dispose of the product, your company will suffer heavy financial losses. Management has asked the new Problem-Solving Team to help you solve the problem of what to do with two million pounds of glow-in-the-dark playdough that comes in four colors.

Refer back to the summaries in your Japanese notebook as you go through the following steps with the other team:

STEP 1—DEFINE THE PROBLEM (IN TERMS OF CONFLICTING NEEDS)

_____

_____

_____

_____

_____

_____

STEP 2—BRAINSTORM POSSIBLE SOLUTIONS

_____

_____

_____

_____

_____

_____

STEP 3—EVALUATE AND ELIMINATE ALTERNATIVES

Read each item on your list. Discuss each and cross off the suggestions that won't work. Eliminate those that anyone finds unacceptable.

STEP 4—PICK THE BEST SOLUTION AND DEVELOP A PLAN

The one possible solution that would work for all of you: _____

_____

_____

_____

_____

_____

A detailed plan for putting that option into effect, including what each of you is going to do and when:

_____

_____

_____

_____

_____

_____

When are you going to evaluate your plan and how will you decide if it's working or not?

_____

_____

_____

_____

_____

STEP 5—EVALUATION: Evaluation can't be completed in this activity.

HANDOUT 43

Broadcast Journalist

PERIOD _____ NAME _____ & _____

You are a writer and anchorperson for the daily news program on your school's television station. Your news team is producing a series of reports on conflict resolution efforts at your school. **You have been assigned to report on the five-step problem-solving process you learned in chapter 6**. It is newsworthy because it is just one of the many techniques being taught at this school to help students cooperate and solve problems in and out of the classroom.

You are limited to a two-minute time slot. Approximately 270 words can be spoken in a two-minute period of time; therefore, your story must be about 250 words long. As usual, **you will write your story in a form referred to as the inverted pyramid**. This approach will guarantee a concise, broadcast-ready story.

The inverted pyramid is a classic newspaper organization of information that puts the most important, the most startling, the most interesting, or significant information in the first paragraph. The second most important points are listed next, and so on, until the least significant information is in the last paragraph of the story. This technique makes it easier to read a newspaper; if you read the first paragraph you get the gist of the story and you don't need to read on unless you want all the details. When necessary, it makes it easy to cut a story short by eliminating one or two of the last paragraphs.

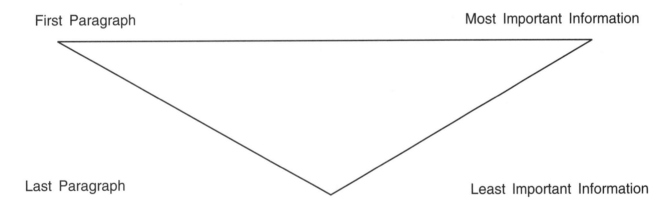

First Paragraph .... Most Important Information

Last Paragraph .... Least Important Information

The first paragraph (the lead paragraph) of an inverted pyramid story summarizes the essential facts of the news item. It answers the five "W's," the Who? What? When? Where? and Why? of the story (and sometimes the How?). These are the basic questions that the journalist tries to answer for the reader in any news story. The answer to any one of these questions could provide the starting point for your lead paragraph. Who? and What? are usually the most significant, and, typically, are used as the starting point of the lead paragraph. Some answers to the five "W's" may be dropped into the second or third paragraphs.

Attach the copy of your story to this sheet when you turn it in.

For extra credit and extra fun: Videotape yourself as an anchorperson delivering your story. Turn in your videotape with the copy of your story.

HANDOUT 44

Essential Questions

PERIOD _____ NAME _____

1. Why is punishment an ineffective response to misbehavior?

    •

    •

    •

    •

    •

    •

2. How does giving children choices and allowing them to experience consequences contribute to self-esteem and responsibility?

    •

    •

    •

    •

    •

    •

3. What are natural and logical consequences and how do they come about?

    • **Natural consequences**

    • **Logical consequences**

4. What considerations should be included when giving a choice?

-
-
-
-
-
-

5. What are the key issues to consider in designing logical consequences?

-
-
-
-
-
-

HANDOUT 45

Collage of Choices

PERIOD _____ NAME _____

A collage is an artistic composition made of various materials (paper, cloth, wood, photos, string, magazine cutouts, etc.).

Use any method to divide your paper in half.

Make one collage illustrating the following idea from chapter 7:

PUNISHMENT IS NOT THE BEST RESPONSE TO MISBEHAVIOR.

Construct your collage to "explain," through the use of pictures and symbols, why punishment doesn't work to correct misbehavior. Use your knowledge of the many reasons why punishment does not promote maturity and responsibility.

For example: You could illustrate the idea that punishment doesn't work because it almost always involves anger. Anger often teaches a child to be afraid of the parent. Acting out of fear is not acting responsibly.

On the other half of the paper, make another collage illustrating the following idea from chapter 7:

GIVING CHOICES AND ALLOWING CHILDREN TO EXPERIENCE CONSEQUENCES WILL ENABLE CHILDREN TO LEARN HOW TO BEHAVE IN THE MOST RESPONSIBLE WAYS.

This collage would show how giving choices and allowing consequences promotes maturity and responsibility. Get inspiration from chapter 7!

For example: Having the power to make decisions gives us a good feeling about ourselves.

Attach this sheet to your collage when you turn it in.

Chapter 7

HANDOUT 46

Compose a Jingle

PERIOD _____ NAME _____

Consequences are the events that result from the choices we make. In other words, they are the *products* of choosing.

For this activity, we're going to say that you work for an advertising agency.

Your job is to think of ways to promote and publicize various products. Right now, you're developing a campaign for a family service agency. They are launching a project aimed at reducing child abuse. Your campaign will consist of public service announcements offering positive discipline alternatives. The objective of the first public service announcement is to promote the use of natural consequences and logical consequences instead of punishment. It was discovered in a focus group that consumers don't know the difference between natural and logical consequences. Your team has decided that a jingle would help *teach parents the characteristics of each kind of consequence and the differences between the two types of consequence.*

A *jingle* is a short verse or song marked by catchy repetition. For example, the Wrigley Company's jingle for Doublemint gum is a jingle. Can you recite it?

Your assignment is to write a jingle that:

- Defines a natural consequence

- Defines a logical consequence

- Gives the key issues to consider in designing logical consequences

_____

_____

_____

_____

_____

_____

HANDOUT 47

Valid Choices—Checklist

PERIOD _____ NAME _____

As you take on more mature roles in relationships (as a friend, co-worker, parent, and so forth), you will need to give choices to others. When giving a choice, remember that a choice must present when, how, or with whom a task is to be done. It states the available alternatives.

Here is a checklist that you can use to identify valid choices:

Checklist for a Valid Choice

_____ The choice states when, how, or with whom a task is done.

_____ The choice considers the age and developmental skills of the child (person).

_____ The child (person) is not given the choice of whether or not to do the task (unless he or she actually *does have* the choice of whether to do the task).

Refer to the checklist to write a valid choice for each of the following situations:

1. It's raining. You want your seven-year old to stay dry on his walk to school.

Example: Do you want to carry an umbrella or wear your raincoat? _____

2. Your two-year old loves to play at the park, but throws sand at another toddler.

_____

3. Your six-year old needs to take a shower. He's having fun playing outside right now. He really doesn't enjoy showers.

_____

4. Your ten-year old's hair is getting long; it seems to be matted and oily all the time. It was so much easier to care for when it was shorter. She isn't taking responsibility for it.

_____

5. You want your seven-year old to practice reading for a few minutes every day. He likes to read but he wouldn't think of practicing on his own.

_____

6. You drive to work with a friend every day. She has been late every day this week.

_____

7. You pick up a friend every day on your way to school. He has been late every day this week. You sit and wait and have been tardy twice.

_____

HANDOUT 48

Responsibility Chart

PERIOD _____ NAME _____

One of the most common areas where parents use choices and consequences is in encouraging performance at home. Performance refers to doing all the things a family member is expected to do. Parents begin to teach responsibility by giving more choices and by increasing expectations for performance. Babies aren't expected to do much but by the age of six or seven, a child might be expected to perform several tasks on a daily basis.

Most children and parents benefit from having a concrete (visible, touchable) list of expectations and some concrete way to show that they have completed a task. A visible record also allows children to see their responsibilities written down and relieves the parent of the need to nag.

Your assignment is to make a responsibility chart for a seven-year old. This chart will be added to your Portfolio. This is a good age to begin the use of consistent expectations. The expectations on a real chart would be tailor-made to the needs and practices of the child who would be using the chart. Furthermore, the child should be included in deciding what his or her responsibilities will be. For this assignment, include the following on your chart:

Morning Responsibilities

- Make bed
- Get dressed
- Come to breakfast on time
- Brush teeth

After School Responsibilities

- Homework
- Household job
- Practice (reading, drawing, sports, music, etc.)

Bedtime Responsibilities

- Put on pajamas
- Clean up (bath, shower, wash face . . .)
- Brush teeth

Design some way for the child to show completion of each task or set of tasks. For example, you could put a Velcro dot next to each item and have large cardboard check marks with a Velcro dot on the back.

The child could place these on the chart when a job is finished. Be creative! Try to develop a chart that a child can do easily, quickly, and independently.

Using a responsibility chart with a child sets the stage for learning about choices and consequences; you are helping the child to see that results are determined by their actions. With young children, you would work with them to carry out their responsibilities; however, at some point a child must take the initiative to choose to perform at home or not. A parent's role is to establish limits. This means that a consequence would have to be connected to the child's choice to perform.

Write answers to these questions and turn your answers in with the responsibility chart:

1. How would you keep track of daily and weekly performance?

_____

_____

_____

2. Describe what consequences you would establish for responsible performance.

_____

_____

_____

3. Describe what consequences you would establish for lack of performance.

_____

_____

_____

Chapter 8

HANDOUT 49

Decision Tree Business Card

PERIOD _____ NAME _____

It would be great to have a copy of the decision tree to refer to in the future when a problem arises. Make a card that you can fold in thirds and put in your wallet. This information might help you while you are living in the dorms at college, in a dating relationship, at work, at home with your family, etc. Laminate your card or cover it with clear contact paper. Make a machine copy for your **Portfolio**.

Cut out the card provided here and mount it on stiff paper. You may decorate the other side in any way—perhaps you can make it look like a business card.

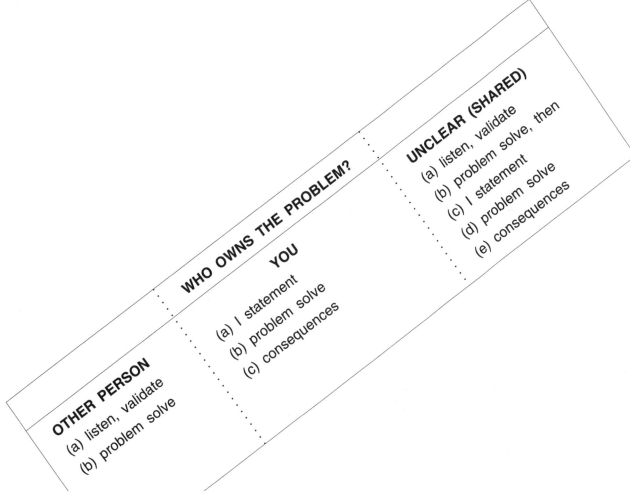

WHO OWNS THE PROBLEM?

OTHER PERSON
(a) listen, validate
(b) problem solve

YOU
(a) I statement
(b) problem solve
(c) consequences

UNCLEAR (SHARED)
(a) listen, validate
(b) problem solve, then
(c) I statement
(d) problem solve
(e) consequences

HANDOUT 50

Essential Questions

PERIOD _____ NAME _____

1. Why is learning to cope with anger important to building relationships, especially the parent-child relationship?

2. Why do we get angry?

3. How do we get angry? What happens that causes a transition from one feeling or state to a state of anger?

4. How can an individual reduce his or her anger?

Answer: Recognizing your trigger thoughts and knowing how to change them are essential parts of coping with anger. Name nine ways to reduce your anger:

Changing What You Say to Yourself—Changing Your Trigger Thoughts

    1.

    2.

    3.

    4.

Changing What You Do—Changing Your Behavior

    5.

    6.

    7.

    8.

    9.

HANDOUT 51

The "A" Collection

PERIOD _____ NAME _____

Record each event that makes you feel angry for the next seven days.

Date	Describe the Event That Made You Feel Angry	Describe the Circumstances Related to the Event (Stressors and Trigger Thoughts)

HANDOUT 52

Aztec Codex

PERIOD _____ NAME _____

A codex is a fold-out book with interesting pictures and symbols. They were created by an Aztec scribe, or writer, and often contained records of history, calendars, gods, and descriptions of the daily life of the Aztec people. You may add drawings or photos to your codex.

Your codex must have the following information on the pages:

Front Cover	Write Your Name, Date, Course Title
Page 1	Write the title "The Two Requirements for Anger"
Pages 2–10	Across the top of all of these pages, write the title "The Nine Ways to Reduce Anger"
Pages 2–10	Write each of the nine ways to reduce anger on these pages. Write one way per page.

Instructions for Making Your Codex

1. Fold the strip of butcher paper like a fan. Make a fold every five inches. You will end up with ten parts or pages.

2. Now, glue the end pieces of the long folded piece of butcher paper to two 6" x 4" pieces of poster board to make the front and back book covers. The book should then fold out accordion-style.

Glue end piece of paper
to book cover

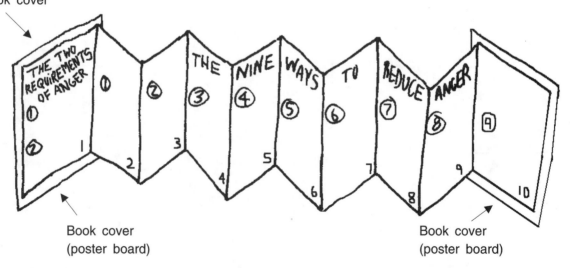

Book cover
(poster board)

Book cover
(poster board)

Chapter 9

HANDOUT 53

Educational Film

PERIOD _____ NAME _____

Video is a great communication tool being utilized in business, government, entertainment, and education. Your team is asked to produce a specific <u>part</u> of an educational film. The goal of this film is to teach people how to cope with anger. Class groups will produce different parts of the film. The parts may be edited to produce one film.

1. **THE TREATMENT:** A brief description of the film. Most of this treatment is done for you; all you need to fill in is the concept you want to communicate.

Audience: High school through community college students and young parents.

Objectives: To produce a video that will

- communicate the negative influence that anger can have on relationships, including violence.

- communicate how anger surfaces as a response to stressful feelings.

- communicate how trigger thoughts ignite stressful feelings into anger.

- communicate nine ways to reduce personal anger.

Concept: The exact information you have been asked to communicate in your part of the video. (It is OK to use words from the chapter.)

_____

_____

_____

_____

_____

_____

_____

_____

Viewing time of the entire video _____ . Viewing time of your team's portion of the video _____ .

2. **THE STORYBOARD**: A storyboard is a series of boxes that tell a story in pictures. When making a video, the storyboard helps you to envision the scenes of your video in advance. It will save you time and help you to not become confused. In your video, these pictures will be acted out by people and their dialogue will communicate the concept further. You could also film the storyboard pictures and have a voice narrating the concept.

Use the boxes below to sketch what you have in mind for your video. Each box represents about thirty seconds of viewing time. Under each box, write a brief description of what you are trying to show (communicate). Later, all parts of the video, made by different teams, will be spliced together to create the final product.

1.

_____

_____

_____

2.

_____

_____

_____

3.

_____

_____

_____

4.

_____

_____

_____

3. **THE SCRIPT**: The script is the dialogue that your actors will speak in the video. It carries most of the concept. If you use still drawings, photos, or pictures, the script becomes a narration spoken by an invisible narrator.

Chapter 10

HANDOUT 54

Essential Elephant

PERIOD _____ NAME _____

After reading chapter 10, write the main points of that chapter on the trunk of the elephant. You will need to add a longer strip of paper to the bottom of this Handout. Most of the important information from chapter 10 is a list of suggestions for ways to nurture yourself. The elephant's trunk is a great place for a long list! This list will become part of your Portfolio.

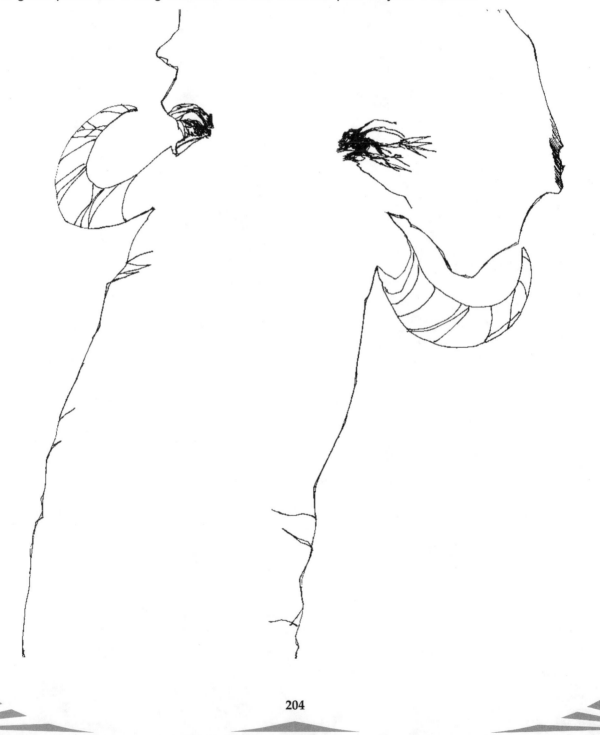

Chapter 10

HANDOUT 55

Community Service Video

PERIOD _____ NAME _____

Video is a great communication tool that has become increasingly popular in business, government, entertainment, and education. Your team has been asked to produce a specific *part* of a simple community service video. Later, all the parts of the video made by different teams will be spliced together to create the final product. The part that you are asked to work on is to help make new parents aware of the need to nurture themselves at the same time they nurture their children. By making this part, you will provide a community service.

1. **THE TREATMENT**: A brief description of the video. Most of this treatment is done for you, all you need to fill in is the concept that you want to communicate.

Audience: Couples and singles attending prepared childbirth classes at a local hospital.

Objectives: To produce a video that will

- communicate the idea that parents need to nurture themselves to enhance their performance as parents
- give them suggestions of ways to nurture themselves

Concept: The exact information you have been asked to communicate in your part of the video (it is OK to use words from the chapter).

_____

_____

_____

_____

_____

_____

_____

Viewing time of the entire video: _____

Viewing time of your team's portion of the video: _____

2. **THE STORYBOARD:** A storyboard is a series of boxes that tell a story in pictures. When making a video, the storyboard helps you envision the scenes of your video in advance. It will save you time and confusion. In your video, these pictures will be acted out by people and their dialogue will further communicate the concept. You could also film the storyboard pictures and use a voice to narrate the concept.

Use the boxes below to sketch what you have in mind for your video. Each box represents about thirty seconds of viewing time. Under each box, write a brief description of what you are trying to show (communicate).

1.

2.

3.

4.

3. **SCRIPT:** The script is the dialogue that your actors will speak in the video. It carries most of the concept. If you use drawings, photos, or pictures, the script becomes a narration spoken by an invisible narrator.

HANDOUT 56

Community Service Display

PERIOD _____ NAME _____

A display can be a great way to get information to the public. Displays must be posted in locations where they are seen by the intended audience and where people have the time to read the information presented. A display can be any size, it can be a simple poster or it can take the shape of a free-standing structure. A display can show information in words, words and pictures, or can be interactive. Think of the displays and exhibits you have seen at museums and fairs.

Your team can create a display for any audience and can display it in any location appropriate for your audience.

Here are some possibilities:

Audience: High school or college students, expectant parents, parents

Possible Display Locations:

- A classroom used for prepared childbirth classes

- A waiting room in a doctor's office, clinic, or hospital

- The infants department in a retail store

- The public library

- The school library or display case

- A teen health center

YOUR PLAN: _____

_____

_____

AUDIENCE: _____

OBJECTIVES: To produce a display that will communicate the idea that parents need to nurture themselves and to give suggestions of the ways they can nurture themselves.

CONCEPTS: The exact information you want to present in your display.

_____

_____

_____

Draw sketches of your display with descriptions of photos, headings, text, and placement of each element.

HANDOUT 57

Feature Article

PERIOD _____ NAME _____

Write a feature article for your school newspaper, a hospital newsletter, or the family section of your local newspaper. The objectives of your article are the following: (1) to communicate the idea that parents (and people in general) need to nurture themselves to enhance their perform-ance, and (2) to give people suggestions of the ways in which they can nurture themselves.

Feature-article writing may adapt some of the creativity of fiction writing while sticking with the basic facts. The information in your article must be accurate, but it can be presented in an imaginative way. You can use material acquired in interviews, a survey, humor, etc. Your feature piece can be two paragraphs or more.

_____

_____

_____

_____

_____

_____

_____

_____

_____

_____

_____

_____

_____

_____

_____

_____

_____

Chapter 11

Handout 58

Application for a Parenting License

NAME _____

Think of all the things a person has to go through to get a driver's license. . . .

- There are many driving laws to be learned from the driver's handbook.

- There are many driving practices to be learned from hours of behind-the-wheel instruction and training.

- There is an age requirement.

- The candidate must appear at the DMV office to take written and behind-the-wheel tests and must pass these tests with a high score.

Driving is a big responsibility because a driver may affect the lives of other people. Our society has established these standards for drivers because we don't want unprepared or potentially dangerous drivers on the road.

Now, think about society's requirements for parenthood. . . . That's right, there are no official standards or licensing requirements to become a parent. Becoming a parent is a basic human right and, as such, should never be governed.

Alas, it is time to pretend. In this final activity you are asked to create an application for a parenting license. This application would be completed by people desiring to become parents. **On your application, ask for the information that you think would be pertinent to establishing the candidate's qualifications and preparation for parenthood**. Use 8½" x 11" paper.

Consider the following:

What background information would be needed about the candidate?

Would the candidate need to acquire training or education prior to applying?

Would there be an age requirement? Some other measure of maturity?

What questions would you ask about the candidate's intentions, abilities, knowledge, skills, family, work, etc.

What agency would collect the applications and issue parenting licenses?

Have fun!

Prepared for Parenting
Certificate

Given to _____

for _____

date _____ signed _____

Plant Parenthood

CARE? HOW OFTEN? WHAT IF IT GETS CARE? WHAT IF IT DOESN'T GET CARE?

What is another word for "care"? N _____

213

OVERHEAD 2

Concept Wall

INSTRUCTIONS for CONCEPT WALL

> You are looking for concepts (ideas) in the chapter that describe the essential components of nurturing and how parents perform nurturing. Don't be shy. Write down anything you find about the component!
>
> You will also need to fill in the lower portion which describes the positive benefits that a child gets from receiving this type of nurturing on a regular basis.

- All the 1's find concepts in the chapter about the first essential component listed—Attention—and write them in the column below that word.

- The 2's find concepts about the second essential component—Mirroring.

- The 3's find concepts about—Understanding.

- The 4's—Acceptance and Respect for Who They Are.

- The 5's—Soothing Their Pain.

- The 6's—Fostering Self-Esteem.

- The 7's—Look for concepts in the chapter that describe neglect. In the lower portion of this section, list the devastating effects that result from neglect.

Beads Of Oman

How to Make Note Cards

Get 6 cards from the teacher.

Write about each component of nurturing on the cards:

> On one side of a card, write the name of one of the components of nurturing.

> On the other side of that card write a few words to describe how to do that type of nurturing.

You will end up with six note cards, one for each component of nurturing. You will place these cards into the silver jewel box you made.

How to Make Your Necklace

Carefully make holes with a pencil on the top sides of your silver box. Run the elastic or string through the holes, and center the box on the middle of the string. Add beads to each side of the box until you have a necklace. Tie the ends of the string together.

Keep the necklace in a visible place in your room to remind you how important it is to nurture others.

Chapter 1

OVERHEAD 4

Notetaking

How To take Notes

Name _____ Topic _____

Period _____ Date _____ # Pages _____

What Time Is It? It's TV Time!

"Notetaking"

Name _____   Topic _____

Course _____   Period _____ Date _____ # Pages _____

Write the name of the component of nurturing that is acted out.	In this space, write brief descriptions of each scene in which the actors play out some form of nurturing.

Flash Cards

Examples

What is a reinforcer?

It is a reward given for a particular behavior. It can be anything that increases the chances that a behavior will be repeated.

SIDE 1 OF 3" x 5" CARD   SIDE 2 OF SAME 3" x 5" CARD

Make a set of FLASH CARDS that will help you organize the information you read in chapter 2. The essential questions are listed below. Write the question on side 1 of a 3" x 5" card. Find the answer and use key words or phrases to write the answer on side 2 of the 3" x 5" card.

Essential Questions:

1. What can we do to encourage children to behave better?

2. What is reinforcement?

3. What is a reinforcer? (See example.)

4. How does positive attention work as a reinforcer with adults and children?

5. Give some examples of ways to give positive attention.

6. Does negative attention act as reinforcement?

7. Give a few examples of negative attention.

8. What might be some outcomes for a child or adult who is constantly criticized?

9. What are the four steps to finding and reinforcing the good?

10. How do parents and children (and people in all kinds of relationships) benefit from finding and reinforcing the good behavior?

No Questions Asked!

Picture 1

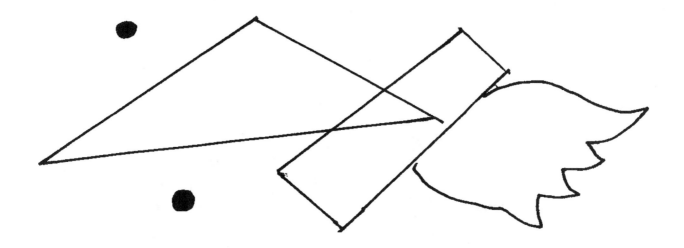

Picture 2

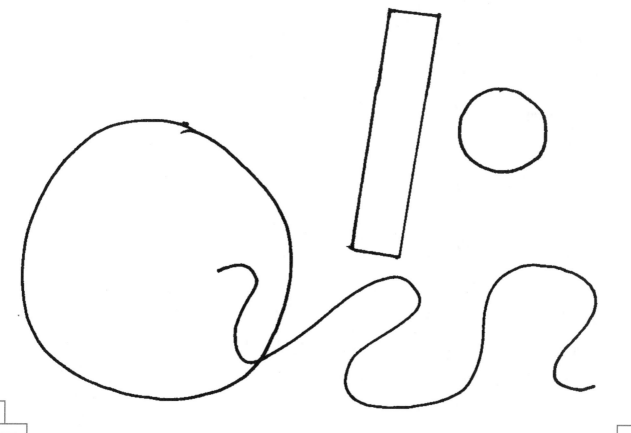

Chapter 3
OVERHEAD 8
Mind-Map Mobile

PERIOD _____ NAME _____

A mind map is just another way to take notes. During or after reading chapter 3, organize the chapter information using the organizer below. You may fill in the mind map with either words, symbols, or pictures.

LISTENING

BLOCKS TO LISTENING

4.

1.

5.

8.

2.

6.

9.

3.

7.

10.

RULES FOR REAL LISTENING

1.

2.

3.

Puzzled About Who Owns The Problem? Completed Diagram

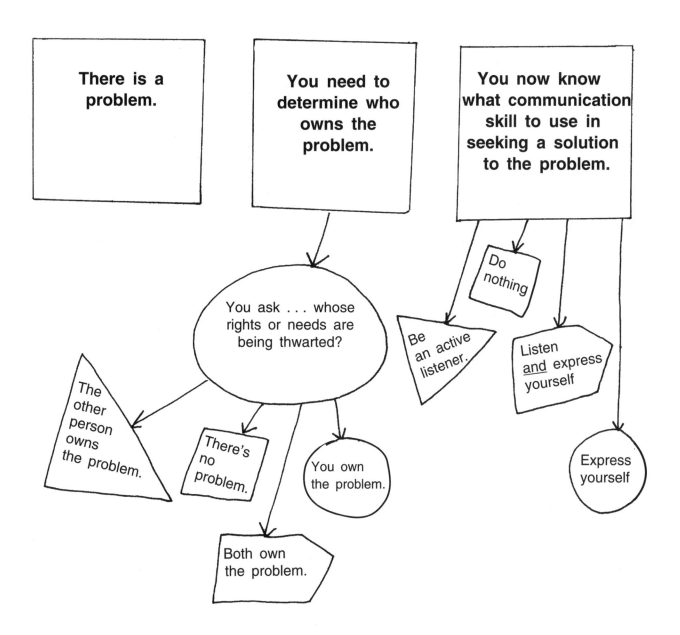

Free Write Topics

The worst decision you ever made.

The best decision you ever made.

A consequence from which you learned the most.

A consequence that brought you happiness.

A horrible consequence that caused you to feel badly about yourself.

A consequence you experienced that taught you the value of something or someone.

A time when you were completely confused and could not choose.

A time when you experienced a consequence caused by a decision made by a friend.

A time when you became a more responsible person because of a consequence you experienced.

Please describe

a. The event.

b. Your feelings about the event.

c. The role and influence of your parents in this event.

d. Examine and describe the lasting impact that the experience had on you.

Chapter 8

OVERHEAD 11

Instructions For Exercise 1

1. Form pairs. Partners will take turns.

2. Use your decision tree business card for reference.

3. Follow these steps:

   1. The first person reads situation 1 out loud.

   2. Use your decision tree business card for reference.

   3. Referring to your decision tree business card, decide who owns the problem and then describe to your partner with which response you would start.

. . . DO NOT READ the example answers until later.

2. Then, the second person reads situation 2 out loud. Referring to your decision tree business card, decide who owns the problem and then describe to your partner with which response you would start.

. . . And so on, until you have discussed all six of the situations.

3. NOW, you can go on to read the example answers given at the end of the chapter and read the chapter conclusion.